OH LORD

I FORGOT AGAIN!

Seven Strategies To Overcome Spiritual Amnesia

KL Ensor

Copyright © 2023 By KL Ensor

www.klensor.com[1]

OTHER TITLES BY KL ENSOR

Milestones, Pillars and Pearls, Bible Study Workbook

Moments with Mom

Most Scripture quotations are from the Holy Bible, New International Version. All Scripture taken from the HOLY BIBLE, NEW INTERNATIONAL VERSION® unless otherwise noted. Copyright © 1973, 1978, 1984 Biblica. Used by permission of Zondervan. All rights reserved. The "NIV" and "New International Version" trademarks are registered in the United States Patent and Trademark Office by Biblica.

Library of Congress Cataloging-in-Publication Data

Ensor, KL

Oh Lord I forgot again/ by KL Ensor

ISBN: 979-8-9886813-0-4

Copy Editor: Melanie Chitwood

Cover design by: EnsorAgape

Note Page by: Tall Poppy Designs

Author photo by: EnsorAgape

Smashwords Edition July 2023

---

1. http://www.klensor.com

All rights reserved. This document or any portion thereof may not be reproduced or transmitted in any form or by any means, electronic or mechanical, without the publisher's express written permission, except for the inclusion of brief quotes in a review.

For Steve, Denyce, and Andrew

NOTE TO READER

Thank you so much for taking the time and spending it with me. I love God's Word. I love teaching. I enjoy talking about the things of God with others. Being the product of two excellent teachers and the oldest of four siblings, I enjoy that I get to teach God's Word and not be in the hot seat. Basically, I get to say *Thus saith the Lord* and just stand and smile, because He said it, and that settles it. No pressure on me, but there will be on all of us if we do not obey, but that's for another day.

"Oh Lord, I Forgot" is a product of a desire to give my Sunday Bible Study a gift for the holidays. I wanted to do a devotional, something small, thought-provoking, and symbolizing how much I love each of the members of the class. As I was praying and thinking, the Scripture Isaiah 55:8 seemed to light up like a marquee on Broadway: "'For My thoughts are not your thoughts, neither are your ways My ways,' declares the Lord" (NIV). This was a reminder to me that God knows what His people need. He alone knows what kind of encouragement, challenge, change, or correction they need. He loves His people, His bride, and His church. Once I remembered it wasn't my job to get people to do what they were supposed to do or called to do, I was able to focus on what God wanted me to do in my writing.

Since my family and I had just finished *40 Days of Prayer* by Rick Warren, I did a little review. Then while sitting in my car thinking about a totally different study topic and lesson, the Holy Spirit gave *"Oh Lord I Forget Again"* to me.

I just thank and praise God for who He is. Seems every time I am having the most difficult or challenging or heart-wrenching situations, sometimes not of my own making, He comes right away and gives me so much more than I need that it overflows.

My eyes are watering now as I remember the day I was about to quit nursing school. My heart was so heavy, and the spirit of depression was trying to grab onto me. I was sitting at my desk waiting for my next class to start. Looking at me no one would have known that I was having one of the worst days of my life. I pulled out a piece of paper and the words just flowed. My poem, "If My Stethoscope Could Talk," was born. It has been published in a national nursing journal. It has been read at pinning ceremonies, and I know at least one of my professors who keeps it on the office wall.

But that is how God works. He takes the hurts, the disappointments, all the ugly, and He makes something so profound and beautiful and amazing we're still in awe years later. So all the glory, honor, and praise belong to Him and go to Him.

If you are thinking you're too old, too young, too hurt, too damaged, too anything, this book is definitely for you. You are still here because the Lord is not done using you. How and what that is is something you need to diligently seek God over. He knows why He created you. He knows what you are good at and not so good at. He knows the desires of your heart. He knows what is perfect for you and how best you can bring glory to Him. So if you think "you can't," then most likely "you won't." But if you allow God to truly grow you into all of your potentials and rely on His strength and His grace, He can turn all those excuses of "too" into opportunities and victories. With God nothing is impossible.

I wrote *"Oh Lord, I Forgot Again"* to encourage, remind, and nurture growth in your relationship with Christ. I hope this will be a resource for you to stand more victoriously as you battle your flesh, the enemy, and as you strive to be more like Jesus. I hope you'll be motivated to let the power of God strengthen you regularly rather than relying on God as an afterthought.

In the following chapters, we'll explore these truths we need to remember:

1. Whose You Are

2. Who Brought You Out

3. The Importance of Following the Instructions

4. The Importance of Knowing Your Calling

5. Recognizing It's Not About You

6. Trusting His Promises

7. Understanding It's Already Done

We can be so forgetful at times and it has nothing to do with age. When we see that pretty ring or golden necklace sitting in the jewelry store, we sometimes forget there was a "process" it had to go through to get there. Gold has to be refined, so it is heated, cleansed, and pounded to get it malleable for forming. I had no idea what soda ash and borax were until I started doing the outline for this book! But those two cleansing agents are important in the process of preparing gold.

We may not always like the things that happen during the process, but they are necessary. I pray that these words are a blessing and an encouragement so we can live victoriously and not fall into the trap of spiritual forgetfulness.

Your Sister in Christ,

KL Ensor

FIRST THINGS FIRST

God Loves You! He loves you so much that when mankind messed up He had a plan in place to fix the problem. The sin that Adam and Eve committed separated us from God. In the old days, a sacrifice had to be made to cover the sin. Jesus came to earth to be the ultimate sacrifice. His holy blood would cover each and every sin for those who would believe in Him. His gift of life through His death would restore us back to God. Salvation is free, it's a gift. Jesus' death and resurrection provided the one and only way of salvation.

The Lord pursues you waiting for you to welcome Him so He can right the wrongs in your life. He is the only one who can. If you have never accepted the Lord's gift of salvation, I'm praying today is the day! Don't delay, tomorrow is not promised and He eagerly awaits your surrender to Him.

The Lord does not make it complicated. First, you must recognize that we all need a savior. "All have sinned and fall short of the glory of God," Romans 3:23. God in His mercy and grace was not going to abandon His most precious creation. "But God demonstrates his own love for us in this: While we were still sinners, Christ dies for us," Romans 5:8. The world will try to bargain away bad behavior or use explanations or other religions to try to take away the guilt of sin. Sin has a penalty and it must be dealt with. "For the wages of sin is death, but the gift of God is eternal life in Christ Jesus our Lord," Romans 6:23.

Once you've recognized that you need Jesus and decide to come to Him, there is something else you get to do. "If you confess with your mouth that Jesus is Lord and believe in your heart that God raised Him from the dead, you will be saved," Romans 10:9. The world will try to make you doubt your salvation. The devil will definitely try to get you to doubt your salvation. At times even you will doubt your confession of faith. Fear not, God Always Keeps His Promises! "For, everyone who calls on the name of the Lord will be saved," Romans 10:13.

"For God so loved the world that He gave His One and Only Son, that whoever believes in Him shall not perish, but have eternal life," John 3:16

Do you believe that? If you answered yes, Hallelujah, and welcome to the family of God! On page 95 I have a list of resources for a New Believer to assist on this blessed new journey!

1

REMEMBER WHOSE YOU ARE

Do you remember the day you accepted Christ as your Lord and Savior? What was that day like? Had something tragic or life-altering happened? Did you go up to the altar because everyone else was going up, and you didn't want to be alone? Did you raise your hand after a rousing sermon from a visiting pastor or during a revival service? Did you choose to receive Christ as your Lord after being away or disconnected from family and those who love you?

When I was nine years old, I was part of a large group of city kids who came together from a variety of nearby churches to do Bible study and choir rehearsal. One day a particular Bible story caught my attention, and on that day, everything changed. Jesus wasn't just a story anymore. I accepted Jesus Christ as my Lord and Savior, and after that, everything seemed distinctively different. The sky seemed bluer than normal. The flowers were more vibrant. I was overflowing with joy and happiness. I couldn't wait to get baptized. Each time I think back to that day, I can't help but smile. What made that day even more special was that it was the same day that my sister also decided to accept Jesus Christ too.

Let's pause for a moment to talk about being christened. If you were sprinkled on as a baby or small child, this is not accepting Christ into your life. Accepting Christ is personal, and it is also something *you* declare. At a wedding, the bride and groom have decided to be dedicated to each other. This decision is personal between the couple, but they also declare their commitment before witnesses. Just like the bride and groom say "I do," so must each person say *yes* to Christ, accepting Him as Lord and Savior, and sharing the decision to follow Christ with others.

Let me pause for another moment to say this: if you don't remember the actual day you accepted Christ or where you were or the surroundings, this will not be held against you. As long as you accepted the Lord as your personal Savior, that is what is important. When you can say that "you know that you know that you know," and you have no doubt that you belong to the Lord, that is what matters. Dates are great for reflection and remembering, but they should never outshine the act of committing your life to Christ.

Whenever that date was and whatever the circumstances surrounding it, the day of your salvation is now the most important day in your life. It's more important than your birthday, wedding day, graduation day, or any other day that's a milestone or an important memory. We tend to miss birthdays and anniversaries, but this "new life" day is one we should never forget. God remembers it. This precious day is important to God and He treasures it. You've just made an eternity decision. This is the day you became His. You need to remember this when your circumstances are tough and challenging.

You especially need to remember *whose* you are because you now have an enemy. Satan, who was ignoring you up to this point, has decided to set his sights on you, and you have become his target. Scripture tells us the enemy comes to "'kill, steal, and destroy' (John 10:10). He does not want you to remember you belong to the Most High God. He doesn't want you to remember you are more than a conqueror (Romans 8:37). He doesn't want you to remember God's faithfulness (1 Thessalonians 5:24).

When we forget whose we are, we can feel homeless and destitute. We begin to live in doubt and fear. We let our thoughts of not being good enough or missing the mark keep us from running to our Father who is waiting with open arms. Just like the prodigal son finally came to himself (Luke 15:17), we also need to have those moments, sometimes daily.

Oftentimes the devil isn't the one trying to sabotage our joy, peace, and relationship with the Lord. Many times we do it to ourselves. When we think we are strong enough, Christian enough, or have been saved long enough, we are operating in our own strength. In Isaiah 64:6 we read that our righteousness is as filthy rags. We are cheating ourselves when we try to use our puny strength. Our minds, behavior, thinking, and our total approach to life have to be changed (Romans 12:2).

Let's look at some ways that will help us remember whose we are.

Get in the Word

Getting in the Word doesn't mean simply reading Scripture. It doesn't mean taking notes during the sermon and never looking at them again. Getting into the Word isn't sitting in multiple Bible studies and collecting folders full of information. Jesus prayed, "'Give us today our daily bread,'" and He was referring to being fed spiritually (Matthew 6:11). So many Christians are malnourished and unhealthy, knowing just a little bit of Scripture. When we need endurance, we will fall short because we haven't bulked up on God's Word. The Word is also necessary for us to hear God's voice and understand His purpose for our lives. 2 Timothy 3:16-17 says, "All Scripture is God-breathed and is useful for teaching, rebuking, correcting and training in righteousness, so that the servant of God may be thoroughly equipped for every good work." His Word is His love letter to us. To truly experience His love we need to get into His Word.

Fellowship with Other Believers

We need to get together with other Christians on Sundays at a regularly scheduled church service. However, we need to include additional time with Believers. When we fellowship with one another so we can encourage each other. Sharing testimonies, victories, struggles, and difficulties is part of what families do. As Christians, we are in the family of God. We have brothers and sisters who can now be prayer partners and Bible study buddies as we grow in faith together.

Do you know why the new church was so powerful and impactful after Jesus left and the Holy Spirit came? One of the reasons is that they were zealous and dedicated to being a body of Believers (Acts 2:46). We need each other! When we are not participating in the family of God, our absence is felt. A body doesn't work well with missing pieces. Feet and toes are just as important as elbows and earlobes.

The Apostle Paul in Hebrews chapter 10 encourages us not to throw in the towel when things are not going how we want them to go when it comes to congregating with others. When Believers get together, we might get on each other's nerves and maybe we won't be best friends, but we still need to function as a unit and be about our Father's business. We only get strong and more united when we come together.

Step Out in Faith

We often hear Christian statements such as this: walking by faith, living by faith, and stepping out in faith. However, if we were to ask Christians what these statements mean, we'd discover many Christians don't know how to explain these when it comes to Christian living. Biblically we are challenged to conduct our lives and make all our decisions based on our faith and trust in God and His Word. We must always seek to trust in God and His promises, instead of trusting in what is seen and heard in our current circumstances. One commentary explains walking in faith this way:

Rather than loving the things of this world (1 John 2:15-16), Christians should spend their lives glorifying God in everything they do (1 Corinthians 10:31). It requires faith to live this way because we cannot see, hear, or touch anything spiritual. When we base our lives on the truth of God's Word rather than on the popular philosophy of our day, we are going against our natural inclinations. (Houdmann, gotquestions.com)

Faith is the substance of things hoped for the evidence of things not seen, (Hebrews 11:1). When we accept Christ, that is a faith move. And then just like a newborn can't stay a baby, it is also true for us as Christians. We have to grow too. How are we going to grow?

Abraham is referred to as a pillar of faith for hearing and obeying the command "go," leaving everything he knew and all that was comfortable (Genesis 12:1-9). He did it again when the Lord told him to sacrifice Isaac (Genesis 22:1-19). Abraham's relationship with the Lord grew stronger as he learned to trust and obey.

When Peter first stepped over the side of the boat requesting the Lord to let him walk on water, he showed confidence in God (Matthew 14:22-26). That took faith. Even though he faltered, we know that wasn't the end of Peter's story, for he goes on to be a mighty ambassador for Christ.

Notice these individuals did not stay in the "infant" stage of their lives. They grew, but it took operating in faith.

For us to grow spiritually, we must step out of our comfort zone and operate in faith, completely trusting God (Proverbs 3:5-6). Whether it is a ministry, lending a helping hand, or sarting a new job, faith needs to be a part of each and every decision. When we allow God to use us, we are stepping out on faith. This takes prayer, prayer, and more prayer. Jesus got away to pray often. He is our example.

Abraham, Peter, and the others weren't perfect. Abraham tried to give God a hand and Peter took his eyes off Jesus and sank. But look what

God accomplished in their lives anyway, despite their shortcomings. The Lord wants to do the same in you.

Practice the Fruit of the Spirit

Another way to remember whose we are is to practice the fruit of the Spirit. The fruit is found in Galatians 5:22-23, "...the fruit of the Spirit is love, joy, peace, forbearance, kindness, goodness, faithfulness, gentleness, and self-control; against such things there is no law."

Merriam-Webster Dictionary defines the word *practice* as the act of doing something again and again in order to learn or improve. We can learn to practice the fruit of the Spirit. We must practice love, not just with the people we like or want to hang around. We must practice joy and praising God. And this cannot be dependent on if we feel like it or not. We have to practice peace and keep our mouths shut and refrain from discussing other Believers and things from their past. It is paramount that we practice forbearance, otherwise known as self-control, restraint, and tolerance.

If you have ever been to the gym or tried a new workout regime, you were probably sore the next day. If you were truly dedicated, you did not let the temporary discomfort keep you from working out again. You kept at it and your body and muscles adjusted, got stronger, and your endurance improved. So it will be when you practice the fruit of the Spirit–you will get stronger. Remembering whose you are will become more natural.

Pray Daily

We read in Scripture to "pray without ceasing" (I Thessalonians 5:2). This is our time to talk to our Heavenly Father and let Him talk to us as well. We've all been in situations where one person is doing all the talking all the time without taking a moment to listen to the person they're unloading on. Sometimes our prayer time can be like this one-sided conversation where we talk and talk without listening to God. We don't want to let our time alone with the Lord just be a time to give Him our laundry lists of wants and desires. Then we just wait for His response like a spoiled, entitled kid, expecting to get what we think we ought to have.

Prayer is a weapon. When we unleash prayer on the enemy, things happen, and things are changed. Even our flesh has to shut up, back away, and break off the attack. I challenge you to have a prayer session that starts with "Lord, thank you, speak to me," and then don't say another word. When we do this, our prayer life moves to new heights.

Memorize Scripture

Remember when you had to memorize your timetables or a list of words for a spelling test? We were taught to memorize our phone numbers and addresses. Many of us memorized speeches from Easter and Christmas. As a kid, I could sing the jingle from a commercial at the drop of a hat—I can still sing the Tootsie Roll candy song from the 80s! Most people have a collection of factoid information that serves little purpose other than to remind us of fun memories and good times. These situations where we've easily memorized things show us that we can memorize Scripture.

Think about the analogy of a bank—you can only withdraw what you deposit. In other words, you only get out of something, what you put into it. What are you investing in yourself? We all have favorite Scriptures and passages, but are they so embedded in our spirit that they are our "go-to"? David writes in Psalm 119:11, "I have hidden your word in my heart that I might not sin against you." Many a Scripture has come to my mind to help me run from temptation and not yield to my designs and plans.

Reading the Word is not enough. Joshua 1:8 tells us to "'keep this Book of the Law always on your lips; meditate on it day and night, so that you may be careful to do everything written in it. Then you will be prosperous and successful.'" As a teacher of God's Word, I naturally spend more time reading as I prepare my lessons. But I keep my study time separate from my personal alone time with God. Jeremiah 31:33 tells us, "'This is the covenant I will make with the people of Israel after that time,' declares the Lord. 'I will put my law in their minds and write it on their hearts. I will be their God and they will be my people.'"

Share Our Faith with Non-Believers

One of my favorite Scripture passages about sharing our faith is found in Acts 8:26-40. Philip, one of the first deacons, received a message from an angel of the Lord to go south on a desert road. God had set up a divine appointment for him to meet a man of great importance that happened to be reading from the book of Isaiah. Philip explained to the man Whom he was reading about. The man accepted the good news about Jesus, and as they came upon some water, Philip baptized the man.

Sharing our faith and our belief in Christ ought to be something we look forward to with *joy*! We should be bursting at the seams trying to share why we're going to heaven and why *everybody* should come along with us and spend eternity. We should be shoving everybody into the car like a stressed-out mom trying to get to church on time with ten children. Alas, it seems to be the first thing Christians abandon and the last thing we want to take on when we're spiritually emotional.

Why?! Why?! Why?! We say we love the Lord. We say we are thankful for all that He has done. Even drug addicts share how they got better. Why are we so unwilling to share the Savior of the world? The Great Commission in Matthew 28:19-20 still applies today, as well as John 3:16, Romans 8:38, and Joshua 1:9. We belong to the King of Kings and Lord of Lords. I'm getting happy as I type these words...I know I'm having a praise break once I finish this chapter!

We must all strive in word and deed to be like Phillip. The Lord said "Go" and the door was barely closed and locked before he was off to make a disciple. I can just imagine Phillip bouncing on the balls of his feet as the Ethiopian read aloud, just waiting for his chance to break the bread of life with a potential new brother in Christ! This is amazing stuff! And we have the Creator of the Universe right in our midst. He wants us to share Him with this dying and hurting world. We must remember Whose we are and then go do some spiritual bragging!

We serve an amazing God! Don't believe me? Read Psalm 19. Our amazing God made us and wants to use us to bring glory to Him as He blesses us while making us a blessing to others. We are His most precious creation. He created us to have a relationship with Him and share His character with others. He has a plan for our life, and we are not a mistake. Never forget whose you are.

Here's a summary of what we learned in this chapter about remembering whose we are.

Get in the Word

Fellowship with other Believers

Step out on faith

Practice the fruit of the Spirit

Pray daily

Memorize Scripture

Share our faith with non-Believers

HEY NEW BELIEVER! What I pray you received from this chapter is that the Creator of the universe loves you and only wants to give the best to you. Read God's Word daily with intention. Seek fellowship with your Christian family. Step out on faith by trusting God with the circumstances happening in your life. Let the Fruit of the Spirit become character traits of your life. Pray each and every day and not just about your wants and needs. Pause and learn to listen for God's voice. As you read each scripture, start memorizing scripture.

Having scripture readily available in your mind and heart will prove beneficial. And finally, share your faith with others. Just like you would show excitement over a new car or job, you now belong to the King of Kings and Lord of Lords. He is the answer to all that is wrong in this world. Reread the last paragraph of this chapter and be encouraged.

2

REMEMBER WHO BROUGHT YOU OUT

You are a royal priesthood, a set apart people. You are bought with a price. In the last chapter, I talked about whose you are. Now let's go a little deeper and talk about *who the whose is*.

The book of Exodus is the story of God delivering the children of Israel from the hands of the Egyptians and bringing them to the Promised Land. This important story in the Old Testament should encourage us and serve as a strong reminder of the powerful God that sees our needs, has a plan to meet our needs, and works everything out for our good. He is a God of details. Unfortunately, the children of Israel tended to be more disobedient than obedient, even after God delivered them in a very miraculous way. God delivers, Israel obeys for a time, then falls into disobedience. Then the consequences of their disobedience overwhelm them, they call out to God, God delivers, and then it happens again. If you were to call the Israelites the most forgetful and ungrateful people of all time, not many would argue with you.

Sadly we aren't too far removed from the same behaviors of the Israelites. *Amnesia* is defined as the loss of memories, such as facts, information, and experiences. I think sometimes God's children walk around with intermittent spiritual amnesia. We act like the Israelites many times. The Lord delivered them, and then they started acting foolishly once they were set up in the land God had promised to give them. In the same way, the Lord comes through for us time and time again, and then we fall into foolishness and forget the details. We act like we have never been delivered, never received a blessing, or like God has not made a way for us.

Consider open heart surgery, more specifically, an open-heart bypass surgery performed under general anesthesia, which requires the patient to be on a ventilator during surgery. The surgical procedure begins with harvesting the blood vessels that will become the grafts. The saphenous vein in the leg is commonly used because it is long enough to create multiple grafts. If the saphenous vein cannot be used, vessels from the arm can be used instead. The left internal mammary artery is used for a single graft and is taken once the chest is opened for surgery.

Once the vein has been recovered, the chest is opened by making an incision along the sternum, or breastbone. The surgeon then cuts the sternum, allowing the chest cavity to be opened, and giving the surgeon access to the heart.

In the traditional CABG procedure, or coronary artery bypass graft, the heart is stopped with a potassium solution so the surgeon is not attempting to work on a moving vessel, and the blood is circulated by a heart-lung machine. At this time the heart-lung machine does the work of the heart and the lungs, and the ventilator is not used.

The surgeon places the grafts, usually by rerouting blood around the blockage. The amount of time on the heart-lung bypass machine is determined by the speed at which the surgeon is able to work, primarily, how many grafts are needed.

Once the grafts are complete, the heart is started and provides blood and oxygen to the body. The sternum is returned to its original position and closed using surgical wire, to provide strength to the bone that needs to heal, and the incision is closed.

Now, I hope I haven't completely grossed any of you out! But think about this: as I described those details of what the medical staff did and all that went into the procedure, what did the patient do? Once consent was signed for the surgery, the patient was present but did not perform the procedure; they didn't call a time-out and didn't administer medication. The medical staff performed the vital procedures to help save the patient's life. The patient benefited but did not actually participate in the process.

In the same way, Jesus did all the work and He wants to bless us with all the benefits salvation brings. I think sometimes we act like we went to the cross. As if we suffered, bled, and died. And then we rose again on the third day, and the spotlight should be on us, the Mega-Christian. No Suga-dumpling, I don't think so. Just like the children of Israel were brought out of Egypt and freed from bondage, the Lord did that for you.

During the holidays we usually do a lot better about remembering. We get caught up in the spirit of the event, especially if there are family events surrounding the occasion. But what about the other fifty weeks of the year? Once Easter and Christmas are over, what are you thinking about or focusing on? Does Calvary get you right there in the tender spot in your chest during the middle of August while you're sitting at the beach looking at the waves? Does Christ's humbling himself as a baby and lying in a manger get you thinking of peace on Earth in the middle of June?

The spirit of those two holidays should truly be in our hearts and minds every day. How do we keep those positive feelings and smiling emotions when the world is falling apart or the opposition seems insurmountable? Sometimes I think about the miraculous event of the children of Israel walking through the Red Sea on dry land. I wonder what my response would be. I guess some of it depends on what age I am or would have been. As a kid, I would have been in awe and probably a bit fearful as I held my dad's hand and crossed through.

As a young adult, I would have still had some awe and fear, but I may have had some doubt about how long this was going to last or worried about what to expect on the other side. As an older adult, I may have awe and fear, but my thoughts about the future may be a bit different. In all cases, there is a little bit of fear, a bit of awe, some doubts, and excitement, but the fact remains that God is making a way, no matter my age or situation.

He brought you out! He will bring you out of the horrible situation you might be in right now. That dead-end job. That loveless relationship. The impossible, He made possible. The unbelievable, He made a fact. The unachievable, He made an eventuality. Isaiah 55:8-9 states that His ways and thoughts are not like ours...ours don't even come close. He purposely did not have Moses ascend to Pharaoh, but took him out to the desert, gave him an education, and then brought him back. God does things in such a way that there is no doubt that He made provision and He is in full and total control.

Let me say that again: God is in full and total control. Nothing that happens in this world escapes His attention. Do not believe for a minute that the bad stuff is just arbitrary and God is oblivious to what is happening. His timetable, just like His thoughts and ways, is not like ours either. He is the Deliverer. He has brought us from various situations and just like the poem "Footprints in the Sand," by Ryan Hart says, "He carries us to safety and keeps us by His side."

So how are we going to combat our spiritual amnesia? How can we keep the Deliverer the main focus, since He is our Savior and Restorer? He is the only One who can be the Author and Finisher of our faith. So here are a few things we can do to help us remember who brought us out.

Forgive Yourself

Say what?! Yes, forgive yourself. You can stop spending all that time at the altar about forgiveness. He has already forgiven you. It's done, it's gone, it's in the past. He holds it against you no longer. We tend to bring up, dig up, and relive our failures. When Jesus reinstated Peter, Peter was still hanging on to his guilt and Jesus was telling him to let that go; there are other things I need you to focus on. Now you can spend your time at the altar for other things.

The enemy wants us to be depressed, despondent, and downtrodden because then we can't focus on anything else, like praying for others, encouraging others, or being about the Father's business. We get to *choose* to forgive ourselves. We no longer are under the stain of sin now that we are covered in the blood of Jesus. I believe a great many ailments would not exist if we said that to ourselves every morning, noon, and night. Forgiveness frees. Our minds can now be tuned toward the things of God.

Reflect on Your Blessings

Now I am not saying get caught up in our blessings. We don't need to add the charge of being guilty of worshiping the blessing and not the Blesser. During our time of meditation, we should practice gratefulness by being mindful of everything the Lord has done, everything He has prevented, and everything He wants to do in us and through us. As the song says, "Count your blessings, name them one by one, count your many blessings, and see what God has done." When we focus on what God is doing, we get our minds in the right place. Depression, anger, and even fear have to flee when we let the things of God infiltrate our thoughts. When we think deeply and seriously about all the ways God is busy in our lives, we keep Him front and center in our hearts and minds.

Forgive Others

Genesis 43 describes Joseph's brothers' second journey to Egypt during a time of famine. This time, unlike their first trip, they have their youngest brother Benjamin with them. Verses 26-30 tell the story of Joseph's brothers presenting and honoring him with a gift. Joseph asks about their father and asks about Benjamin, the baby brother. Then in verse 30 we read, "Deeply moved at the sight of his brother, Joseph hurried out and looked for a place to weep. He went into his private room and wept there."

Powerful! This is one of my favorite portions of Scripture because if *anybody* had cause to hate, a cause to want revenge, seek after it, and get justice, it was definitely Joseph, Jacob's son. His older brothers hated him so severely that they wanted to murder him. Family drama at its finest or worse. Fast-forward several years. Not only did Joseph move past his trauma—not just at the hands of his family but at the hands of an employer as well—he is now second only to Pharaoh.

Some of us would be waiting on that passage of Scripture where Joseph rained down ultimate fire and brimstone for the horrible treatment he received. But Joseph continues to show himself as the type of guy we want all our daughters to marry. Not only did he *not* do what so many of us would have yielded to the temptation to do, but he was moved to emotional tears by how full his heart was for his family. Joseph was not allowing *all* the harm done to him to dictate his next moves. Oh, the family reunion that happens when Father Jacob rolled into town!

When we let it go, as the *Frozen* song says, we are now no longer in bondage to bitterness, grief, or any other negative and nonproductive emotion. Forgiveness is powerful and freeing. This is why what Christ did on the cross is so profound and far outweighs what any other religion could ever try to offer to humankind. Plus, God demands that we forgive others as He has forgiven us. (see Colossians 3:13 and Matthew 6:14-15)

Encourage Yourself

Now before you get mad at me for adding more to your spiritual checklist for living with joy, it is important that you recognize that it's not someone else's job to be your personal cheerleader. When you have no other god before the Only Living God, your relationship should be moving in the direction that when you are talking to yourself in the mirror, you're actually talking to the Lord, not yourself. Not sure where to start? Go back to #2 and reflect on your blessings. Read the book of Psalms aloud. Sing to the Lord. This is taking mediation and reflection and putting it into action. Your behavior, what you say, and what you do now demonstrate what you are thinking. If the culture-driven world can inspire self-talk and self-motivation, just think how much more thorough spiritual, Holy Spirit-driven strengthening and restoring is and what it will do once you do it. 1 Samuel 30:6 and Philippians 4:13 are great starters.

Practice Praise

Praise means to "revere (with extended hands), laudation, specifically a hymn, to kneel, and to bless God." Here are a few examples of the biblical use of the words in question:

Deuteronomy 10:21, "'He is the One you praise; He is your God, who has done these great and awesome things for you which your eyes have seen.'"

Jeremiah 20:13, "Sing to the Lord! Give praise to the Lord! He rescues the life of the needy from the hands of the wicked."

Pick a psalm, any psalm, and you have an excellent example of praise.

Psalm 75:1, "We praise you, God, we praise you, for your Name is near; people tell of your wonderful deeds."

I always feel better when His praise is on my lips. Let's put a definition here because many do not always understand what praise is and what it is not. David praised. Paul and Silas praised. We enjoy praise just like we like good news and pleasant sounds. Most people, even if they may not necessarily be vocal, do like hearing joyful and uplifting music and sounds. If you're not a singer, read the Word out loud. That's praise. Make that joyful noise! Feeling shy? Start in the shower. Next, try it while looking in the mirror. Before you know it, you'll be praising in the kitchen, the living room, and all over your house. This will make praise second nature. You'll be able to "have church" anywhere, at any time, during any and all situations.

Worship in Everything You Do

Worship is another very misunderstood word. We call our church services worship, or we use it to describe a church event, but worship is so much more than that. Worship is an attitude and an action. Don't you just love those words that are nouns and verbs?! When we worship the Lord, we adore, revere, and esteem Him reverently and obediently. We are called to love the Lord with all our heart, mind, body, and strength and present ourselves as a living sacrifice (Mark 12:30, Romans 12:1).

Worship is not just a Sunday event. It's not just going through the motions so we can check off some spiritual list. It's also not just sitting around thinking positively and/or being optimistic. Our life, no matter what is going on, is reflective of our total dependence on the Lord and His leading and guiding.

One way to help our lives be an example of worship is to start each morning by asking the Lord, "How can I honor You today?" Not only will He mark out our steps and provide, but He'll also bless us. My Scripture to encourage myself and remember to worship in all I say or do is Acts 16:16-40. Paul and Silas had been proclaiming the Good

News when they met a young female slave that had the spirit of telling the future. She followed Paul and Silas around stating that they were servants of the Most High God.

After several days of this, Paul finally had enough and told the spirit to leave her in the name of Jesus Christ. And the spirit did. Her owners were not happy about that, for they had lost their money stream. Her owners had Paul and Silas locked up, saying that they were advocating unlawful customs. So Paul and Silas were stripped, beaten, and thrown in prison. And to throw salt on the wound, the jailer was told to put them in the inner cell and lock their feet in the stocks or restraints. But Paul and Silas didn't argue over the injustice or demand their rights. Verse 25 says, "About midnight Paul and Silas were praying and singing hymns to God, and the other prisoners were listening to them."

Paul and Silas demonstrated true worship. Their motivation was evident. Their true feelings of adoration and love for the Lord showed. They didn't let their current situation dictate their response, and they worshiped God through it. And since they did not let their current storm push them off course, salvation would come to the home of their jailer.

Surround Yourself with Worshipers

Are you familiar with the phrase "You are what you eat"? How about, "One bad apple spoils the barrel"? (I promise you I was not hungry when I penned this!) Many times we start off really good with praise and we even make a good dent with worship, but then spiritual disinterest happens. By spiritual disinterest, I mean the song leader or choir has to almost beg someone to clap their hands or say hallelujah.

I understand that life is not always nice, sweet, and enjoyable, but let me ask you this…Has God left you? Has God kicked you to the curb? Has God not been faithful? So you have to get with other Believers and talk about the goodness of Jesus. You have to be a part of testimony service and not just an observer. As steel strengthens steel so we must encourage one another, regularly. This is not something to be done alone or rarely.

I did a Scripture search to look for the word *worshiper*, and I was hard-pressed to find one when keeping to just the NIV and King James versions. Every Scripture has worshipers, plural! Now you might start alone, but you won't remain that way. Being with other worshipers is infectious, in a good way! Caution, this does not mean to surround yourself with "yes men" either. This is about authentic worship. Remember God is not looking for a showy, emotional, on-display-for-all-to-see type of worship.

The Lord is looking for genuine and authentic prayers (Matthew 6:5-6), sincere repentance and submission (Luke 18:13), and individuals ready to humble themselves to be the type of worshipers the Lord is seeking (John 4:23-24). If you're worshiping to impress, you're just a sounding brass, and I'm going to have to ask you to take a seat. Christians trusting God wholeheartedly can't help but look to engage in worship that only pleases God. (See also Exodus 34:14; Psalm 85:9; Psalm 103:11; Psalm 119:63; John 4:23)

As we close this chapter, here are the bullet points to help you remember who brought you out:

Forgive yourself

Reflect on your blessings

Forgive others

Encourage yourself

Practice praise

Worship with your life

Surround yourself with worshipers

Notice for each point God is the motivator. He brings people into your life—He provides and makes a way. He forgives and gives you the strength to forgive. God is an awesome God. He desires a relationship with you! You are His and He has no plans of letting you go. The price has been paid. Your ticket is purchased. All debts are canceled. God has brought you out and provided passage. Let this be a daily reminder of His great love for you.

HEY NEW BELIEVER! The Children of Israel or Jewish people as we know them today are God's chosen people. To keep things simple, God chose these unique individuals to introduce Him to the rest of us. I don't know what it was about them that made God want to use them to be His ambassadors but He never makes a mistake. The Jews got caught up in the title of God's Chosen and unfortunately, things have not gone well for them. They didn't do their job and God in His mercy and grace continues to love them but now He calls all of us who He has redeemed and set free to share the gift of salvation with others.

I refer to many individuals from the Old Testament, the book of Exodus in particular, to drive home the fact that God brought you out and is the only One worthy of your love and devotion. To help you remember that fact, forgive yourself and forgive others. Let go of your past and things from your past. God has forgiven and told you to sin no more. Don't let the past dictate to you. Reflect on your blessings. You are not what you used to be and God is not done with you. The sections of this chapter are to help you encourage yourself. This is where memorizing scripture comes in. Allow praise to set your attitude and mood so that everything you do and are involved in become acts of worship as you spend time with other worshippers. May you hunger and thirst for the Lord, Who brought you out.

3

REMEMBER TO FOLLOW THE INSTRUCTIONS

Any product you purchase will come with an instruction sheet, booklet, or manual detailing the step-by-step preparation and proper use of the item. Every Lego set I've purchased has come with instructions. If something seemed out of alignment or wasn't fitting together just right, I could refer to the instructions and correct the problem. Or if I thought something was missing, I could again refer to the enclosed instructions and make sure I had everything I needed.

God's Word is His heart written out for us to learn from and be sculpted into the masterpiece He commissioned us to be. The Bible is not some old, outdated book with information that is no longer relevant today. Let me say that again—the *Word of God* is relevant, never gets old, and always has current application. It will not go out of style no matter what generation tries to disregard God's love letter to humankind. If you are not comfortable with the word application, the employment or utilization of the Word of God is vital to having a true relationship with the Lord.

So many people do not realize it is to their detriment when they do not take God's Word seriously. Christians risk serious spiritual anemia and malnutrition when they do not read God's Word. They fail to grow and will never experience a Spirit-filled life. Also, it's not just about reading God's Word. We have to study it. Study, study, study. I'll talk more about this in a minute.

When asked what my favorite Scriptures are, I am hard-pressed to name just one. I have favorites for the different seasons in my life. Some of my favorite Old Testament Scriptures are about describing the Word of God such as 2 Kings 22:1-23:30 and from the New Testament,

Hebrews 4:12. One talks about how precious God's Word is, and the other demonstrates the fullness and all-encompassing presence of the Word.

Everything we need to live for God and to live with others is in the Bible. Yes, addiction, fornication, stealing, lying, pride, jealousy, and divorce are included. I recall a song the choir used to sing in the church when I was a kid, "Look, it's in there, right in the Word of God; everything you need; I found it all, I found it all, I found it all in the Word of God." I especially liked this song because in the bridge were Scriptures, helping me memorize the verse and the address (address means where the Scripture can be found in the Bible). So let's get to the tips to help us remember to follow the instructions.

Read God's Word Daily

I can't stress this enough. Have you ever tried to put something together without using the instructions? Just when you thought you were done, you take a look at your work and something didn't seem quite right. You had to seek out the instructions so you could correct what went wrong or fix the error. Oh, what needless pain you wouldn't have had to bear if you'd just gone step-by-step in the first place. I feel like I haven't eaten when I miss my daily devotions, and, of course, trouble always seems to come knocking when I have missed my time in the Word.

The distractions were just ridiculous when I wanted to start a family devotion time. I thought barriers were bad when trying to have my personal time with the Lord. Well, the enemy tried really hard to ruin things and keep me and my family from getting in the Word together. I think that's why Sundays seem to be so hard for some people. They can get up and be on time for a doctor's appointment or even a job that God blessed them with, but getting to Sunday School or church service seems to be a hardship. Oh, if Christ had acted the way we do when going to the cross, I wonder if He would have made it. Again, we must pray for the Lord to put a hunger and a thirst for His Word in us, if it isn't already there, especially if it is not something we are passionate about. Most people would give me the side-eye if I dumped 1,000 Lego pieces in their lap and said to build it without giving them the instructions. We have to have a map to know where we're going. We can't use the map very well if we never open it up and read it.

Pray Through It

We must pray before we read Scripture. We can be prayerful while we are reading a passage of Scripture and pray once we are done so the Lord can open up our understanding of His Word. I remember the first time I heard someone pray a Scripture. This was nothing new as many Scriptures we know and love are prayers.

However, as a kid, I had never thought about praying Scripture, especially during a church service. Now, as an adult, praying Scripture has been huge in my life, especially during those times when I didn't have the words or my heart was so heavy I couldn't even stay focused. Thankfully, the Lord knew my heart, hurts, haunts, and hindrances. His Word was just the source of strength I needed to overcome and get back on track.

Study the Word

A Berean is someone who is not satisfied simply hearing God's Word but actively searches the Scriptures for all that is being said (see Acts 17). God does not want us to be the type of Christian that just accepts whatever is said to us. Instead, He wants us to actively and passionately study for ourselves to make sure the woman or man of God is being led by God in their preaching and teaching. We need to stop right now and ask God to give us the desire for His Word. Studying God's Word takes us deeper than just a superficial reading and cursory glance. The act of study makes the subject a part of us. When asked a question, the answer will come naturally, almost second nature. When tested, the solutions involuntarily present themselves. The Word of God will produce spiritual growth and maturity in us without struggle. Remembering Scripture will be like breathing; it will be so much a part of us, certain parts will flow out of us naturally, like instinct, because we'll be actively wanting to do His will and not our own. Studying also encourages intimacy. When we actively research what will be pleasing to the Lord and earnestly look for ways to obey, not because of obligation but because we love Him, we are drawn even closer to the Lord.

Meditate on the Word

This is an area where many of us fail. You might think, *How can you say that, Kim? I memorize Scripture, so I'm at least thinking about Scripture, right?* Meditation should turn into motion. We must not just hear the Word, but we must also do the Word. This makes reading and studying even more profound. The world will convince us to just do the "feel good" Scriptures, but true meditation will put us right smack in the middle of Psalm 51 or one of Jesus' parables that makes us do some serious self-reflection and correction.

We read, "All Scripture is God-breathed and is useful for instruction, for conviction, for correction, and for training in righteousness" (2 Timothy 3:16). In the book, *God's Power to Change Your Life,* Rick Warren puts it this way, "**Meditation** is thought digestion. **Meditation** does not mean that you put your mind in neutral and think about nothing. **Meditation** is thinking seriously about what you are reading. You take one verse and ask, 'What does this mean for my life?' Talk to yourself about it, and talk to God about it."

Share God's Word

I have a question for you: When was the last time you shared a Scripture you've read with someone else? One of my many reasons for loving Bible study is the opportunity to share Scripture. As much as it would seem a good idea to raise your hand during the sermon to ask a question or share support commentary, this is the minister's time to share what God has shared with him/her with the audience present. Small group fellowships and disciplining classes are also great times for Scripture sharing. It's like family mealtime where everyone sits at the table together and shares in the feast. Now that's talking to other Believers. What about non-believers? New converts? Those questioning and seeking? Again, sharing Scripture is a time to bring guests to the table to taste the fullness of the Lord. But before you invite a guest to the table, you have to prepare, wash your hands, set the table, and make sure there is room for all who might show up.

This is where my personal study and meditation time comes in. My prayer is that the Lord will make my heart sensitive to His leading and then say what He wants to be said. By having tools like the Roman Road or the Salvation bracelet at the ready, you'll be able to share meaningful Scripture as you open up the conversation to share the Love of Christ.

Sermon Time

The basics of a sermon are this: a Scripture is read, then the preacher proclaims, "Thus says the Lord." Then the church is fueled up to run on for the Lord another week. Well, that's a simplified version of how it should go. I'm not including this helpful tip to absolve you of personal responsibility or to say you should just do everything that comes from the pastor or preacher.

Also, don't disregard this section. Our life is a sermon, whether we get up in front of an audience or not. We may never read a Scripture or say something longer than five minutes to a crowd of people. But we are called to be a living witnesses in all the Lord does and says in our life. Sermons can be a blessing to the body of Christ when the speaker is sharing what God has given to them during their time of preparation. Also, this is an opportunity to dive into a book of the Bible or a Biblical topic you may not have thought about.

Sadly, some pulpits have turned into arenas of opinions, wishful thinking, and spiritual oppression. Ministers are picking Scriptures and trying to make them agree with them instead of rightly dividing the Word and making sure their lives agree with Scripture. I've heard individuals complain about the "fire and brimstone" sermons, and I've heard just as many complaints about the "it's sunny all the time" sermons.

In all things, there must be a balance because just as God is a God of love, He is also a righteous and Holy God. Sin must be dealt with. We will get into this more in later chapters.

Study with Other Believers

We need our own personal study time, but we also need dedicated time to study with Believers. As much as I love Bible study and have a huge affinity for Bible studies in general, we technically do not need more. If you are over the age of forty and have been in church in some fashion, there have always been Bible classes. We have been given the basics we need to live a Christian life and continue our sanctification journey. Where we go wrong is we don't go deeper. We read it, we participated, we have the workbook and the t-shirt, but that's it. It will sit around getting dust just like our Bible if we don't motivate ourselves and each other. Studying together can also turn into praying together. Where two or three are gathered, Jesus is also in the midst, and we want Him in the middle of everything we are involved in (Matthew 18:20).

Instructions are there to help us and be a road map on our journey. Everything that we need is available and ready to use. We just have to practice looking at the map, making God's Word our Go-To and Only-To.

Here's a summary of what we can do to remember the instructions.

1. Read the Word daily!

2. Pray through it

3. Study the Word

4. Meditate

5. Share

6. Read again "Sermon Time"

7. Read again "Bible Study Time"

HEY NEW BELIEVER! I mentioned the Roman Road and Salvation bracelets and these were items usually received in Sunday School, Vacation Bible School, and Bible camp by kids to help them learn about salvation. They are great Google inquiries. Wrapping up this chapter, before you gave your life to Christ you probably were living by your own rules. You were independent and you followed an agenda you made for your life. Following god's instructions isn't about following rules. The Lord wants a relationship with you. He provides the guidance you need so you can grow and handle His blessings. You must daily read the Word and pray about everything going on in your life. You must study and meditate on the Word, this makes it even more personal. Sharing the Word with others is an important part of your Christian journey. Hearing the Word of God from one of His ministers is beneficial to your refueling so you can be challenged and motivated to spend more time with the Lord. Lastly, you have to study some more.

You want God's Word to be second nature. Join a Bible study to be able to partner with others as you yield to God's Word molding and shaping your life.

4

REMEMBER YOUR CALLING

In chapter one I shared a portion of my story when I accepted Jesus Christ into my life. At the age of nine, there were many things I didn't know and understand, such as how a person is called or what it even means to be called. Depending on your spiritual background or denominational history, how a person is called may vary and look different. Even the term "called" may have a different definition or meaning for you. From what I remember as a child when a person said they were called, they were usually referring to preaching or being a pastor. I can't say with certainty how some of the individuals I watched growing up stated they felt called to be a preacher. I was too young to understand some of the things that were said or shared. I do recall a pastor would take a few individuals under their wing and ordain them according to their denomination's by-laws and regulations. Most, if my memory serves me correctly, did some sort of seminary, and if they did not, there seemed to be some sort of covering or in-house education by the pastor that mentored them as they worked toward being ordained. At this time not many females were included in this group, so I am unsure how the process proceeded, though the process is usually completed with the person preaching their first sermon.

In my older teenage and young adult years, I was exposed to missionaries being trained and sent out. These individuals were prayed over and sent to various places around the world. Most missionaries that I met were comprised of couples where the male was the preacher or pastor and his wife was his helper. At this time in my life, I also learned about students attending a Christian college or university and actively working to be sent outside of the United States to minister. I once applied and was accepted to a Christian school not far from where

I grew up. I visited the campus and loved the idea of going to chapel and being in a Christian environment. I couldn't afford the tuition, but it was always something I wanted to do.

While visiting the campus I attended various workshops that introduced me to women and men excited to fulfill God's will in their lives. During these get-togethers, I regularly heard individuals stating this was when the Lord spoke to them and they answered "the call" to go, do, and be obedient to God's will. Most described how they heard the Lord and what they did next.

I spent an afternoon investigating the words *called* and *calling*. When my online research didn't provide much, I turned to the *Holman Bible Dictionary* to see if there would be any variants from what I'd seen so far. When it came to the Old Testament, I found five different definitions:

To invite, summon (Genesis 3:9)

The call of God to pray, calling on the name of the Lord (Jeremiah 10:25)

Naming (Genesis 25:26)

God calls by name with a view to service (Exodus 3:4-22)

To call one's own, to claim (Isaiah 43:1)

And for the New Testament:

Referring to the Christian life as a calling (2 Timothy 1:9)

Further callings to special ministries (Acts 13:2)

So let's first address the statement of having a calling on our life. The human race for centuries has asked these questions: Why am I here?

What am I here for? What is my purpose? In our teenage years and beyond we might ask, what am I going to do with my life? Then as the middle age years progress we might ask, what am I going to do with the rest of my life? In 2002 when Rick Warren's *The Purpose Drive Life* was published it replaced the current best-selling *Left Behind* series among Christian readers. The book's large success demonstrated even with our advances and increased knowledge we are still asking some of the same questions surrounding purpose and fulfillment.

We all have a call on our lives. All of us. It looks different for each of us. Just as we are unique, we have a unique calling that coincides with the general calling to make disciples (see Matthew 28:19-20). We must first do the original call of sharing the love of Jesus with everyone in all we say and do. Next, we must consecrate ourselves to the Lord so that we might learn what He specifically wants us to do with our gifts, skills, abilities, and talents while living out the Good News in our lives. We all have a role in communicating God's truth to others. Dr. Charles Stanley puts it this way, "He [Jesus] never intended for the disciples to keep the truth of His Word stored away in personal reservoirs of knowledge. Instead, He instructed them to give away all they received from Him. He commands us to do the same."

I've taught enough Sunday School and Bible study classes to understand that having a specific calling on your life is no easy task and it should never be taken lightly. One of my favorite calling stories from the Bible is found in First Samuel chapter 3. Young Samuel is in bed asleep when he thought Eli was calling him, but it was, in fact, the Lord. The verses from First Samuel jump out at me as little Samuel travels from his room down the hall to Eli's, waiting to be instructed on what to do. Many whom I have met in my small time on the planet have wanted an experience like Samuel's to either confirm or solidify the call on their lives. I have also met others who know they have a calling on their life but have run from it. We'll talk about that in another section of this book. Remember God wants to speak to you.

With that said, let's focus on the personal calling on your life. Let me be one of the first if no one else has voiced this to you, "I am so excited for you and how the Lord is going to use you!" Even if I never meet you, know that I am daily praying that all of us will be all that God called us to be. You have a calling on your life. If you don't believe that, start right now saying that to yourself every day. From here on out I'll be pointing to the "one thing" God has special for *you* to do before you leave Earth and go home to be with Him. Again, this is unique to you, and God has everything prepared for you to bring glory, honor, and praise to Him.

If you have ever attended an ordination service or been to a service where a preacher received their ordination or license, it is a moving experience. To me, it seems like accepting Jesus Christ as Lord and Savior all over again.

The word *ministry* becomes more than just some word in the dictionary. It is taking what you teach, speak, and preach about to an even deeper level. It's not just something you do on Sunday (well, it's not supposed to be something you just do on Sunday.) Many think that only the" called" are those who "lead" out front. There is a large collection of Believers that do not understand that they have a call on their life. It may not be to preach, teach, or sing. It could possibly be a divine appointment at a specific store at a specific time to share the love of God. It may be to start a foundation or work with individuals that are marginalized or deemed unessential. Whatever God has for you to do, "Trust in the Lord with all your heart and lean not to your own understanding; in all your ways submit to Him and He will make your paths straight," will become your anthem (Proverbs 3:5-6).

Before we get into knowing your calling, let's take a little sidebar. No one's calling will look like someone else's. Don't start comparing your story. Don't try to recreate another person's story in your life. You are not to look exactly like someone else. You were never intended to look like someone else. The Lord rarely goes about things the way we think He should, so get rid of those thoughts right now. The Lord may remind you in a room with thousands or at a prayer meeting of ten. Never covet another Believer's journey. Just like Moses' ministry doesn't look like Daniel's which doesn't look like the Apostle Paul's ministry, so will your ministry look different from your fellow brothers and sisters in the Lord. Now with that said how are we to go about remembering, or for some, discovering, the calling God has on our lives? How can we take things beyond just being a church attender or on the church membership role? Ready to no longer be a passive participant in the family of God? Let's go!

We Must Listen

We have to be like little Samuel, "'Speak, for your servant is listening'" If you didn't know, hearing is not the same as listening. Nope, not even close. I can hear a noise but do not truly know what the noise is until I actually listen. Hearing is unintentional whereas listening is intentional. I repeat, listening is intentional. By applying the steps you just read from chapters one, two, and three, you are preparing your heart as well as your ears to listen for what God wants to share with you. You are being intentional. You want to know. You desire to know. You don't "hear" the Lord say love and just run out and get married. You listen to His entire message to you about love and then go and forgive that family member that has hurt and betrayed you.

This area has been misunderstood so much. Individuals start out in ministry and then fall away or fall completely out because they say they heard from the Lord but then didn't listen. It is imperative to know what God wants and not try to tweak the frequencies when God is saying something we may not want Him to say to us or that we may not want to obey. Scripture warns, "Let the wise listen and add to their learning, and let the discerning get guidance" (Proverbs 1:5).

We Must Pray

Once you've listened, it is time to pray. Now this kind of praying is not in the category of *if I remember* or *I'll get around to it later*. This is not the memorized prayers or what we say before we bless our food. Not that the Lord can't speak during those types of prayers, but this kind of prayer takes place when we are seeking the Lord on what to do and how to be a blessing. The prayer stance is like the woman who swept her entire house just to find one small coin. She wasn't going to stop until she found what she was looking for (Luke 15:8).

The word *supplication* comes to mind when I think of this kind of praying. These prayers are on the level of Daniel, Hananiah, Mishael, and Azariah. Consistent, consistent, consistent. Their praying was second nature. When they prayed, you knew they were tapping into the power of God that comes from being obedient. The Scripture, "pray without ceasing," had not been written yet but these young men, who had been taken from their homeland and forced into a foreign culture, demonstrated what a strong prayer life can do.

Some years ago someone asked the question, what would happen if men prayed? My answer—read the book of Daniel and you'll see what a transformational prayer life can be like. You'll also see God coming through in a mighty way, again and again and again. Daniel 1:17 says, "To these four young men God gave knowledge and understanding of all kinds of literature and learning."

We Must Seek Mentorship

We need to get a mentor or ask the Lord to direct us to a brother or sister that is strong in the Lord. I want to be careful here because some appear strong but are not and vice versa. So don't seek out a mentor based on appearances. It is not easy asking for help. It is not always easy asking for advice. It is equally not easy to share our desires and dreams with others. Part of my process for writing this book was to get a team together to read with me, pray with me, and have a conversation about what the Lord had laid on my heart to share. It was a struggle. Criticism, constructive or otherwise, can be hard to accept. There is a reason Proverbs 27:17 encourages us with "as iron sharpens iron, so one person sharpens another." It is necessary.

The Lord has already set aside just the right spiritual partner to be with you on this journey. He has it all set up to make sure you will be all He wants you to be. While you are doing all your praying, ask the Lord to make you open to receiving whom He wants to send in your life to assist, strengthen, encourage, and pray with and for you. Scripture reads, "Plans fail for lack of counsel, but with many advisers they succeed" (Proverbs 15:22).

Dedicate Yourself to Life-Long Learning

You must decide to become a life-long learner. This could mean going back to school or possibly an internship or apprenticeship. This puts even more emphasis on the need for spiritual mentors. Spiritual education may look like a traditional university or seminary, or it might be attending a Bible study instead of teaching it.

I can testify that each time I was a teacher, I did receive instruction as well, but the focus will be different when you are just a student and only a student. While you are seeking the Lord about the call on your life, you need to have a student heart, a teachable spirit, and a humble attitude. Teachers should have those too, but I'll address this in the next chapter. Students listen up. You don't know it all and you're not going to. One of the pressure relievers is that God does not require you to know everything. That's His job. He gives you just what you need when you need it.

I want to stop here for a moment and add a little side note: Please do not misunderstand that your calling can only be connected to a traditional school or a degree program. Not even close! Just like the anointing has nothing to do with age, denomination, ordination, or district license, neither does your calling. If you never get any of those things, what God says about you and His sending you are the ultimate authority. Nothing we humans try to say or do will ever stop His plan. God will use whom He wants to use. God will provide the way if schooling via seminary or other education is needed. God does the qualifying, no degree, certificate, or license will ever beat God's endorsement. We always start with seeking God: "'First seek the counsel of the Lord'" (1 Kings 22:5).

Prepare to Wait

Psalm 27:14 says, "Wait for the Lord; be strong and take heart and wait for the Lord." So now for the hard part. Waiting. God sees no need to send us a memo about His plans. Along with our call to make disciples, we are called to be ready. This means waiting is not a state of doing nothing. You are continuing to pray, and continuing to seek the Lord's face and will for your life. Isaiah 40:31 says, "But those who hope in the Lord will renew their strength." This time of waiting is going to be vital in helping us to do the next two steps, but most importantly this time will allow us to truly seek God first and His righteousness. We will be able to organize our priorities and set our boundaries. Our goal is to have the heart of God for His people.

Serve with Gratitude

There is a reason why the Lord will say "good and faithful servant" when we see Him. It is because He desires us to serve. When He emptied Himself of all glory and came to earth to be a sacrifice, He served while He was here. That means we too are to serve. During our waiting and praying we need to be serving. I love the story of the individual that started at the bottom of the company, like the mailroom or reception, and worked their way up. We need to do this within the church, in our communities, and in our homes. It's taking "I got to do" into "I get to do." Our hearts will cry, *Lord, You bled, died, and rose again for me. I want to do as much as possible to show my love and appreciation for Your gift of life.* Consider the Apostle Paul who admonishes us to "serve wholeheartedly" (Ephesians 6:7). Jesus was our example. Everywhere He went He served. He looked forward to doing God's will and we should do the same.

Offer Praise to God

Praise God for what He is doing and what He is about to do. In Acts chapter 16 Paul and Silas, while sitting in the deepest part of the prison, were having church like they had received their release papers. This is not the time to have a sad face just because your ministry doesn't seem to be taking off like you think it should. I once was asked to sing special music at church. I was pregnant with my first child, and no one told me there is the potential to be very emotional. Well, I basically cried through the whole song. I was mortified. I have been a singer for a large portion of my life and there is such a thing as presence and presentation—not that I was performing for anyone, but I still didn't want to look crazy in front of the congregation. Many people said they were blessed by the song I sang. From that day on I understood God can take those things we think are not good enough or what we think are not worth paying attention to and bring a blessing. Praise Him that He is always on time as He molds us, makes us, and shapes us to look less like ourselves and more like Him.

In Joshua chapter one God is installing Joshua in as the new leader of the children of Israel now that Moses has passed on. I love this chapter because every other verse is "Be strong," "Be courageous," "Don't fear," and "Don't be discouraged." Verse nine asks a question, "'Have I not commanded you? Be strong and courageous. Do not be afraid; do not be discouraged, for the Lord your God will be with your wherever you go.'" The Lord has got us. He knows why He's called us. He knows how best to use us.

I'm going to wrap this chapter up with this: maybe at one time you answered God's call but let life and its distractions keep you from walking fulling in His power. We see in these Scriptures how Jesus calls Peter, and how He calls us: "When they finished eating, Jesus said to Simon Peter, 'Simon son of John, do you love me more than these?' 'Yes, Lord,' he said, 'you know that I love you.' Jesus said, 'Feed my lambs'"(John 21:15). The Lord will go on to ask Peter two more times, allowing for reinstatement and restoration from when Peter had denied the Lord.

Possibly you didn't value the call God has on your life and took some things for granted. Perhaps you knew that there would be a sacrifice and so you ran the other way like Jonah from the call the Lord has for you. Fear not—we serve a God that revives, rejuvenates, reestablished, and repairs. Just as He received the prodigal son (Luke 15:11-19), so will He receive you and set you back on solid ground. God's mercies are new every morning just for that reason.

Here is your list to aid you in remembering your calling:

Listen

Pray

Get a spiritual mentor

Learn

Wait

Serve

OH LORD I FORGOT AGAIN!

Praise

Lord, I pray right now for those who are still hanging on confidently, for those who have doubts, for those who are at a crossroads. I pray that You would mark out their steps and surround them with Your encouragement to submit to You, trust You wholeheartedly, and obey Your commands. Thank You, Father, that You "can do immeasurably more than all we ask or imagine, according to Your power that is at work within us" (Ephesians 3:20).

In the mighty Name of Jesus. Amen

HEY NEW BELIEVER! Before truly understanding your calling, you have to first learn to listen for His voice. God has chosen you for a specific purpose. Now the only way to truly know His voice is you have to get into His Word. Study to show yourself approved (2 Timothy 2:15). This will be important because you will need to keep your eyes on Jesus. Not on someone else's gift, talent, or ministry. Pray and listen. Wait, pray, and listen some more. Don't compare yourself to others. Pray for God's Will in your life. Pray to be drawn closer to the Lord. Pray you'll not let comparison cause havoc on your brain. Use this time to build a good habit of alone time with God and gain a better understanding of His plan for you.

5

REMEMBER IT'S NOT ABOUT YOU

In the original version of Roald Dahl's *Charlie and the Chocolate Factory*, specifically, chapter six entitled "The First Two Finders," Mr. Dahl is very descriptive of the children. For those not familiar with the story, it's a story about a chocolatier that has hidden golden tickets inside the candy bars that he makes. Whoever finds the golden tickets will be invited to the chocolate factory. There is a big prize at the end of the tour but only one child can win.

Mr. Dahl begins to describe the first finders of the golden tickets. The first is a boy who likes to eat named Augustus Gloop. The second is a girl named Veruca Salt, and her father was in the peanut business. The father explains that when his daughter wanted one of those golden tickets, he went into town and bought all the candy bars he could get his hands on. Mr. Salt continues, "But three days went by, and we had no luck. Oh, it was terrible! My little Veruca got more and more upset each day, and every time I went home she would scream at me, 'Where's my golden ticket! I want my golden ticket!' And she would lie for hours on the floor, kicking and yelling in the most disturbing way. Well, sir, I just hated to see my little girl feeling unhappy like that, so I vowed I would keep up the search until I'd got her what she wanted. Then suddenly on the evening of the fourth day, one of my women workers yelled, 'I've got it! A golden ticket!' and I said, 'Give it to me, quick!' and she did, and I rushed it home and gave it to my darling Veruca, and now she's all smiles, and we have a happy home once again."

When the Lord first gave me, "*Oh Lord, I Forgot Again,*" I wanted to start the book with this chapter. Had I had it my way, this chapter would be full of carefully crafted criticism of the Veruca's of this world. If we were in a Bible study setting, I would kindly ask you not to point at yourself as certain situations came to mind that would be labeled your Veruca episodes. Equally, I would not have you give examples of the Verucas you've had to deal with. We have all either been or have dealt with people who believed the world revolved around them, and they truly believed themselves legends in their own minds.

Well, I'm grateful to an amazing God that knew I needed to let Him direct how this book was going to unfold. He already knows that people are self-centered and selfish. Just as He didn't send Jesus into the world to condemn it, my services are not needed to be judgmental and self-righteous. The Bible gives plenty of examples of people who thought a bit more highly of themselves than they should have. From a couple pretending to be super spiritual and generous (Acts 5:1-11), to a king who was jealous of a shepherd boy (1 Samuel 19:1), to an entire group of people who thought they were going to build a tower up to heaven (Genesis 11:1-8). We have always thought of ourselves as important. Look at any alien or invader movie and humans must always defeat the enemy and shine as the winners. If any current psychology publication had statistics that narcissism was at an all-time high, I would agree.

The sinful nature that we received from the debacle in the garden guarantees that our first thought is ourselves. From an early age, we are asked about our plans, goals, and dreams. I used to love watching television shows, such as *Kids Say the Darndest Things,* because it is one of the few times the answers are truly honest.

Now as adults, we need to be honest about ourselves. Many of us have crafted our life agendas and have tried to write them out with a Christian pen but they were not in line with God's will for our lives. We tried to add a little church-this and a little ministry-that but it hasn't come close to what the heart of God desires. In a radio sermon I heard some years ago, the minister described a young person that wanted a certain career for their life but God was moving them to do something that "seemed" unrelated and out in left field. Finally, the young person submitted and obeyed the Lord's leading. Once that happened the young person not only got what God had for them, but the Lord also gave them the desires of their heart in their chosen career. Remember where I said God loves to bless His kids? He does, but He doesn't bless us so it can be about us. He blessed us so our focus is drawn back to Him. He blesses us so He can be lifted up and draw more of the lost unto Himself. We must stop making our own plans and then try to get God to endorse them.

Recently I had a conversation with my husband where I told him I felt a little cheated out of some of my young adult years. I don't know who started it and how it became popular, but it seemed groups were teaching success in terms of life goals, the American dream, or The Plan. What was included was you get into a good university, you pick one of the top ten professions of that time, you marry another professional person, and you buy that house in that neighborhood after having the fancy wedding. Then you buy the status symbol car and then the kids come while you manage debt, diet, and daily adult life. I know for the inner-city kids this was to encourage education, but at the churches where these programs had a lot of prevalence, I don't recall any class or workshop about praying about the school you want to go to, praying about your potential future profession, praying about and for your spouse, or not going into debt to get to what God's will for your life should be. At least not to the same level as education and excellence were pursued.

I take some of the responsibility for believing in a world design that was wrapped in a couple of Christian principles and ideals. I wanted to be successful and I wanted to look successful. I wanted that nice house with the pool and the *Good Housekeeping* kitchen. I wanted that luxury car and to be able to go on that trip and not be worried about credit card debt. The world looks at status and flashiness.

Unfortunately, many well-meaning Christians have picked up that bad habit. I am definitely not saying it's a bad thing to have nice things. No way, I still wouldn't mind that car, but when I stopped making my life about my wants, desires, and impressing others and began yearning to know what God wants and desires, those nice-to-have things no longer factor in my decisions and choices. Except for our mortgage, we give praise to the Lord that we are debt free. The Lord has allowed us to not have to live paycheck to paycheck and we're able to be generous with the gifts and blessings He has given us. God has not blessed us to be caught up in ourselves or become spiritual snobs but to give praise and honor to Him for what He had done. He has empowered us to encourage someone else who is struggling or going through a hard situation that He can and will bless you too.

Still not convinced that it's not all about you? Consider how God operates. It's not the kings and leaders that are making a name for themselves. It's the shepherds and runaways that He uses. He doesn't need your money, title, or education. God is not impressed but what people are impressed with.

God is a God of the still, small voice. God is a God of the mustard seed. God is a God of child-like faith. God is a God of using prostitutes, kidnapped children, and broken people to accomplish His greatness.

You are not supposed to be worthy because He will make you worthy. You are not supposed to be all cleaned up because He will clean you up. You are not supposed to have your act all together because He will be the one to create the new and get rid of the old. God always sets things up so only He can receive the credit and be praised.

I did a Google search for a biblical story about a selfish person. I was curious about what the search would bring up. I have to say I was not quite expecting Genesis chapter four. Here is what Google said, "**Cain** is the one who was overtaken by a self-centered attitude and ended up committing a horrible sin. Cain's heart was not centered on God and he didn't care about his brother. He only focused on how he felt and killed his very own flesh and blood."

We've become just as guilty as Cain when we want the church to be run our way, or be the boss of a program, or just plain want everything done our way. Our hearts must be open to the leading of the Holy Spirit and then we follow what He says to do. Our suggestions are not needed. My heart breaks when we are selfish with the Gospel because we are caught up in how we look and sound. Church has become more about Christians being served than us going out and serving.

But there's hope! Jesus Christ provided the example. Philippians 2:5-11 tell us how were to imitate Christ's humility. I love verses six and seven, "Who, being in very nature God, did not consider equality with God something to be used to his own advantage; rather, he made himself nothing by taking the very nature of a servant." He didn't make it about Himself; He made it about the Father. Now in turn we make it all about Jesus because of the amazing sacrifice He made for our redemption.

Remember in chapter 4 where I said students need to be teachable? I extend that to teachers as well. Teachers, leaders, ministers, and all types of positions of authority. We must keep a humble spirit as we serve, even if we are deemed the "expert" in a certain area. Recognizing we can't possibly know everything and that someone else can bring up something we may have missed is important. It is not about us. You had to be a beginner at some point. God has allowed growth in you so you can now encourage someone else's growth. Don't get caught up in your title. Remember you are saved to serve.

We must daily battle not making this life all about us and what we want. First John 4:19 says, We love Him because He first loved us. When we personalize this Scripture we then can say, we obey because He first obeyed the Father. We serve because He first came to serve. We can even extend Jesus' obedient posture to praying, trusting, and waiting. Jesus did nothing outside of the Father's will. He put all focus on God and bringing glory to Him. We are now tasked with that same model of behavior. Each of these reminders serves not just to encourage us spiritually but to keep our focus on the Lord. Remembering "Who brought us out" and "Who we are in Christ" helps us grow in our love and gratitude for Jesus Christ. Remembering to "Follow the instructions" and keep in mind the calling God has on our life. This will provide opportunities to target our attention on the kingdom business of having a heart for the lost and serving others no matter the cost.

So how are we going to do that? As I list these tools or aids, please use them to help you put the Lord's will first in your life. None of these are more important than the other. You must be flexible to how the Holy Spirit will manifest them in and through your life. With every list in each chapter of this book, ask the Lord how He wants to use these helpful tips to bring you into a deeper relationship with the Lord. Are you ready? Here we go!

Spiritual Gifts

Let's look at what Scripture says about spiritual gifts:

There are different kinds of gifts, but the same Spirit distributes them, there are different kinds of service, but the same Lord. There are different kinds of working but in all of them and in everyone it is the same God at work. Now to each one the manifestation of the Spirit is given for the common good. To one there is given through the Spirit a message of wisdom, to another a message of knowledge by means of the same Spirit, to another faith by the same Spirit, to another gifts of healing by that one Spirit to another miraculous powers, to another prophecy, to another distinguishing between spirits, to another speaking in different kinds of tongues, and to still another the interpretation of tongues. All these are the work of one and the same Spirit, and he distributes them to each one, just as He determines. (1 Corinthians 12:4-11)

I'm starting with this because so many are confused, frustrated, or triggered by them. Some denominations are known more by the gifts than the Gift-Giver and that ought not to be so. Romans 12:3-8 tells us not to think of ourselves more highly than we ought to, but we are to be diligent in using the gift or gifts that He has graciously given to us. With every speaking engagement, each Sunday School class, and every presentation, I've always strived to give the Lord my best. I would pray that someone would get saved, and if everyone in attendance were already Christian, then my prayer would be that they mature and grow. I'm glad to be used by God, but I am equally excited to be praying for the new preacher or minister while they are saying "Thus saith the Lord." I may not know the song, but I'm listening for words that help me reflect on what the Lord has done for me. The sermon may not be addressing a current issue in my life but I start praying for others in attendance that may be struggling.

Verse seven of 1 Corinthians 12 says, "Now to each one the manifestation of the Spirit is given for the common good." Read it again. Read it again—this time aloud. Now underline it. Highlight it. Find every Bible in your house and read, underline, and highlight that verse. Your personality and talents beautifully accompany the gifts the Lord has given you, but they aren't about you. Your gifts are to bring glory to God. We all have a gift. We all must decide if we are going to use that gift to glorify ourselves or the Lord. Daily examine your heart, mind, and spirit about your intentions. Is it about you being in the limelight or lifting up Jesus?

We've allowed charisma and stage presence to take the place of anointed and Holy Spirit-filled use of our gifts. Spiritual gifts must be used in concert with prayer and worship. Otherwise, we're just emotional, happy motivational servers that are strongly looking like people-pleasers with a positive message. So do not get caught up in your gift. And please as I mentioned in the last chapter about your calling, do not compare the gifts either. The Apostle Paul wisely listened to the Lord when he wrote the love chapter (1 Corinthians 13) placing it smack dab in the middle of chapters twelve and fourteen. Notice he taught about spiritual gifts, cautioned us to love and be guided by love, then continued talking about the use of gifts of the Spirit.

I'll let Dr. Charles F. Stanley have the final comment on spiritual gifts, "at the time we come to faith in Christ, every Believer receives at least one spiritual gift-not merely to encourage and build up our own relationship with the Lord, but to edify the entire church. God makes us interdependent because He never meant for Believers to 'go it alone' in their walk of faith but to enjoy the amazing blessings of fellowship with Him and others."

Fruit of the Spirit

As a kid, I mistakenly said the *fruits* of the spirit. I mean, Galatians 5:22-23 lists nine virtues. Isn't there a rule for pluralizing where there is more than one? Of course, with my childlike understanding, I believed that I would get those things in my life and then become a stronger, healthier Christian. We have all prayed a prayer, such as, Lord help me love, Lord help me be more patient or more kind. I am not saying stop praying for the Lord to continue making and shaping you, but I want to lovingly suggest something since this Christian life is not about you.

First, the only thing we should be pursuing is Jesus, not these virtues. Second, these virtues were not meant to show our level of dedication and resolve to the faith, just like keeping the ten commandments didn't show a close relationship with the Lord. Thirdly, you cannot yield fruit. Nope, you can't. Now the Holy Spirit can produce fruit and then we can bear it. I love how God lovingly puts us in our place.

The fruit of the Spirit demonstrates that we need to be dependent on the Lord. That we must daily and constantly seek the Spirit's leading and not pretend to be perfect. The Lord is sanctifying and transforming us. When we come to that realization, we are less likely to be discouraged when we make a mistake. We know He is there helping us to progress in our growth and turn from our selfish wants and desires.

In John 15:5 Jesus says, "'I am the vine; you are the branches. If you remain in me and I in you, you will bear much fruit; apart from me you can do nothing.'" When we focus on Jesus and not ourselves, the fruit of the Spirit is produced. We must be singularly centered on Christ and Him alone. Our sinful nature won't let us make these qualities on our own…they would probably be mutants anyway. So, it's not your peace; it's His peace. It's not your love; it's His love. It's not your self-control; it's His. Again, I'll share some wisdom from Dr. Charles Stanley: "When we are completely reliant upon the Lord and obey the promptings of His Spirit, they [fruit of the Spirit] flow from us freely and draw other people to Him."

The Commandments

Do you ever wonder why the Lord gave Moses the ten commandments (Exodus 20:1-17)? If God knew we couldn't keep those commandments, why did even go through all that effort? I remember

OH LORD I FORGOT AGAIN!

learning them in Sunday School, and then grinning even harder when Jesus gave us two in the New Testament. I'll speak more about Jesus' commandments in a moment. Do you ever wonder what was God aiming for by giving us something in many ways is and was impossible?

Honestly, I would have been the boring Israelite because I like checklists and having guidelines to keep me on track. I would not call myself a goody-two-shoes, but I must say I like not being in trouble. If God said it, I'm good. I am okay without having any elaboration on big issues. Yes, there are certain little things in my life I would love Him to explain, but His reply each and every time is "Trust me." Not everyone can or is comfortable with doing that. They need their whys, hows, and what-fors before they even give the rules serious consideration.

No matter how hard I try I always leave one of the original ten commandments out or I paraphrase it somehow. The first four I got down flat since they pertain to God. The other six, I might get them out of order a little bit when I say them from memory.

We find the commandments in Exodus 20:1-17:

1. You shall have no other gods before me.

2. You shall not make for yourself an image in the form of anything in heaven above or on the earth beneath or in the waters below.

3. You shall not misuse the name of the Lord your God.

4. Remember the Sabbath day by keeping it holy.

5. Honor your father and your mother so that you may live long in the land the Lord your God is giving you.

6. You shall not murder.

7. You shall not commit adultery.

8. You shall not steal.

9. You shall not give false testimony.

10. You shall not covet anything that is your neighbor's.

The King James Version starts these verses with "Thou shalt not." No ifs, ands, or buts, you are not to break any of God's laws. The first four commandments are about God. We must put Him first. Intimacy with God is a top priority. God first and then everything else falls into its proper place.

This then leads us to the other six that govern our relationships with others. Obey these and your relationships with others will be blessed, not perfect but blessed. Note, these are commands, not suggestions. Also, note that following these with the same attitude as not speeding on the freeway keeps you away from trouble and heartache.

Jesus fulfilled what we could not do in our strength. In Matthew 22, we read about Jesus teaching in parables. Instead of the religious leaders of that time seeing the unique opportunity to seek in-depth and profound meaning in their religious lives, they set out to trap Jesus with their words. Jesus, the Teacher of Teachers, knew exactly how to respond to these supposed experts. In verses 37 to 40, He gives a thorough answer that again points to the importance of obedience and not being in bondage to traditions and rules. We read, "Jesus replies: 'Love the Lord your God with all your heart and with all your soul and with all your mind. This is the first and greatest commandment. And the second is like it: Love your neighbor as yourself, All the Law and the Prophets hand on these two commandments.'"

God was not being mean or unreasonable. God was putting into action His plan to correct what Adam and Eve had corrupted. We needed instruction. We also needed to see that we needed God and in and of ourselves, we come up short. Commandments point out that there is a requirement on our part.

Witnessing

In 1921 scientists from the University of Toronto were the first to find a way to produce insulin from pancreas cells without destroying the cells. In 1928 Dr. Alexander Fleming returned to his laboratory and found a contaminated petri dish. If he had thrown it out instead of investigating the unique results, we might not have penicillin. Another important discovery came about in 1941 when a Swiss engineer noticed he and his dog were covered in tiny barbs from the cocklebur plant. He noted the tiny hook-like burrs that snagged on his clothing and dog's fur. After ten years of working with fabric, he would patent Velcro. As wonderful as these inventions and discoveries are, they wouldn't mean much if they had not been shared.

Sharing information has two barriers. One is fear of ridicule and embarrassment, and the second is fear of having our discoveries stolen by someone else and not getting credit for our hard work. Praise God that sharing His love and the blessing of salvation are not attached to monetary gain. I don't think Christians suffer from the second fear, but the first one keeps many quiet and unwilling to participate in making disciples. Not only do we do a disservice to the lost, but we also miss out on opportunities to grow and be blessed.

In Matthew 28:19 we read, "Therefore go." This eliminates all excuses, all reasons, and all explanations. *But Lord, I'm shy. But Lord, I'm not all together yet. But Lord, what if they ask hard questions? But Lord, the room was too cold. But Lord, I don't have the right type of clothes. But Lord, I don't speak the language. But Lord, I don't know the culture. But Lord, I don't have a bad enough redemption story. But Lord..but Lord..but Lord.* Please realize, not one of these will stand up in the court of the Lord.

You have the cure! You are going to get blessed whether you speak like a seasoned orator or stumble and stutter through the words. I shared how my crying through a song spoke more than if I'd given a Grammy-winning performance. What comes from the heart reaches the heart. Jesus wants us and desires for us to share Him. We are saved to serve. I don't want to overwhelm the listener when I share Jesus. I must pray for balance when sharing the love of Christ. I don't want to overshare or downplay what God has done for me. Love, joy, peace, and kindness become evident when I share Jesus.

The right outfit is not needed. Special formatting is not needed. A stage is not needed. Perfection is not required. The Samaritan woman had been saved all of five minutes before she was going and telling the entire village (John 4:4-26). She didn't have hair and makeup at the ready. The PR team hadn't handed out flyers. She just shared her testimony. She still wasn't all Jesus wanted her to be, but she was a precious person that communicated God's work and not her mistakes. Just a willing heart submitted to the Holy Spirit's leading during a divine appointment to rescue another one from eternal separation.

We read in Matthew 9:36-38, "'When he saw the crowds, he had compassion on them, because they were harassed and helpless, like sheep without a shepherd. Then he said to his disciples, 'The harvest is plentiful but the workers are few. Ask the Lord of the harvest, therefore, to send out workers into his harvest field.'"

I pray we start having an urgency about sharing the Gospel at all times. I want to have people hanging off the Train to Glory because there aren't any more seats. Or do you feel like heaven is at capacity and no further work on your part is needed? This world is hurting. People are dying without the Savior. Let today be the last time you didn't shine your light for Jesus. Don't worry about if they say yes or not, right now. Just share the message. Some might, and others won't. I purposely have not unfriended anyone on my social media. Some have let me know they have no intentions toward the saving grace of Jesus. I smile and know that Jesus has saving and redeeming intentions toward them. If something I say or share plants a seed, glory to God!

The Apostle Peter wraps this section up, "With many other words he warned them; and he pleaded with them, 'Save yourselves from this corrupt generation.' Those who accepted his message were baptized, and about three thousand were added to their number that day" (Acts 2:40-41).

Giving

I always like the song, "You can't beat God's giving, no matter how you try; the more you give, the more He gives to you." I have seen how generous God is time and time and time again! I love giving, and if I can do it in secret without my name being on it, I love that even more! My family knows this for a fact. My church family knows this for a fact. People at my job know this for a fact. The sneakier I can be about it the more I want to do. And it's not just about giving money. It's also about giving my time, my knowledge, and my talents. One year I had something going on every month. All were prayerfully considered because I didn't want to be guilty of the sin of being busy. God blessed everything He directed me to do.

In Acts Chapter 5 we read about Ananias and Sapphira, who were all about making themselves look good in front of the church family. We might call them the super spiritual couple. Dr. Luke tells us that Ananias and Sapphira sold some property and together decided to act like the money they were bringing before the apostles was the full amount. However, they had secretly kept a portion back for themselves. I'm not against philanthropy, and, Lord knows, I don't need a pew, let alone a building, named after me. Unfortunately for some people, it is all about the accolades and gestures.

Acts 4:32 states, "All believers were one in heart and mind. No one claimed that any of their possessions was their own, but they shared everything they had." So there was no reason for Ananias and Sapphira to do what they did. Some give to get the tax credit. Some give to "look" like they care. Some give so they don't have to physically, emotionally, or mentally engage.

As a private person, I won't naturally have everybody and anybody over to my house, except for when the Spirit directs. That still does not excuse me from sharing all I have with others. It might be a listening ear, a hug, or a smile. It might be explaining the importance of taking all your antibiotics as directed by the doctor to help with an infection or just how beneficial water is. It might be monetary or spiritual.

Sometimes giving can be quiet. A few years ago the Lord commanded me to be quiet. I was to *not* point out the obvious or leave a note with a Scripture lying around. I was giving certain individuals the opportunity to grow. Can't keep the training wheels on forever. It was a great learning time for me because it showed I can give myself in praying for someone else just as richly as offering advice or writing a check.

How we give also points back to our calling and our spiritual gifts. Whew, God is so awesome and amazing! He's already got it built in for us to give when we just trust Him and obey. I'll wrap this section up with 2 Corinthians 9:7, "Each of you should give what you have decided in your heart to give, not reluctantly or under compulsion, for God loves a cheerful giver."

Fellowship

Growing up in a church that had something for all ages, including Sunday School and Vacation Bible School for all ages—yes, even the adults, fellowship was not a hard thing to achieve. Church anniversaries and pastor appreciations allowed for even more fellowship with visiting churches and choirs in attendance. Potlucks were always a favorite, and the Easter and Christmas programs always brought everyone together. Now outside of church fellowship was not always so cut and dry. I was fortunate to go to school with many I also attended church with. We didn't always hang out and we weren't best friends, but I could sit with them and not feel like the odd man out.

As I got older and grew into young adulthood, fellowship became a little harder. School, work, professional obligations. Being involved in choir helped make sure there was fellowship. It also brought to light that it is important to have these relationships with your brothers and sisters in Christ. You know the pastor will pray for and/or with you, but who else do you have on your prayer warrior speed dial? My husband told me once when I was in the hospital that there was another church member in the hospital as well, and half the church took up the entire waiting room. He said by the time he was able to get a seat in the waiting room, I was already headed to recovery.

I pray we all have connections like that, but we have to fellowship to get them. We must spend time getting to know each other. If we look at any chapter in the book of Acts, we can see they knew how to fellowship. They wanted to fellowship and looked forward to it. They didn't want to leave from their time together. Is that the state of your heart? Do you look forward to time with the family of God with excitement or dread? Not only do we need to be around God's people, but the church family also needs that opportunity to be able to lay hands on us, pray over us, and sing praises to God with us. Even though there is a "you" component, notice God loves making all of us a "we."

An effective Christian is not an island. We find in Scripture God's instructions about fellowship: "Let us hold unswervingly to the hope we profess, for He who promised is faithful. And let us consider how we may spur one another on toward love and good deeds, not giving up meeting together, as some are in the habit of doing, but encouraging one another-and all the more as you see the Day approaching" (Hebrews 10:23-25).

Obedience

Yes, the Lord brought us right back to this one, as I told you at the end of the commandments section. Everything is a verb; something you do. We are to use our gifts and be used by God to bear the fruit of the Spirit. The commandments are the prescription, but the prescription doesn't do us any good unless we take the medicine. Obedience is taking the medicine. Enough of just reading about what we should do; it is past time to do what we have read. We must witness, we must fellowship, we must give, and we must obey His commands. I asked earlier in this chapter, why did He give the commandments? Because He wanted us to choose obedience. If you don't hear anything else from this chapter, hear this, "Obeying God is essential to pleasing Him." Obeying God should be the principle we live by.

God loves you! God desires to be in your life. He is committed to you. I am humbled all over again as I type these words. Our sinful nature wants to tell God that we know better than He does when it comes to life and situations. Disobedience is not pretty, hence why those of us who are parents are not happy when our kids do not obey. I love my kids, and I want what is best for them. My rules are meant to keep them out of trouble and to help them make better choices that will have positive consequences. If you're not a parent but a manager and have subordinates, there is a certain expectation that the rules will be followed. If not, discipline will have to be given. God's commands are much more important than any rule we humans can come up with. Plus everything God does for us always leads to life.

Ask yourself the following: Will obeying God cost me more than disobeying Him? Can I experience greater happiness by committing this sin than I would by obeying God? God does not give us commandments because He wants to control us; rather, His commandments prepare us for His blessings (Stanley). By obeying the Lord more and our selfish nature less, we become too busy to complain about our circumstances. We don't have time to compare what we have to others. We won't have time to criticize others for not being what we think they should be. We will be more concerned with pleasing God and having others see what a blessing it is to be His.

So here is our chapter round-up to help us remember this life is not about us:

1. Use your spiritual gift for God's glory

2. Allow the Holy Spirit to bear the fruit of the Spirit in your life

3. Reflect on God's commandments

4. Witness in all you do and say and share Jesus

5. Give cheerfully of all God has blessed you with

6. Fellowship with other Believers

7. Obey God, obey God, obey God

Lord, this was a tough chapter, even for me because we all tend to think more highly of ourselves than we should. I know You desire for us to lift You up so You can draw all people to You. People we may not readily associate with. People we may not miss being on the planet. People who will never be in our inner circles. With that said, this does not have to be a tough chapter. You want us to lean and depend on You. You desire to strengthen us so You can use us. So much awaits us when we stop trying to be the king of Your kingdom. Help us remain in You, Lord, that we might bear much fruit, showing ourselves as Your disciples. In Your Name. Amen.

HEY NEW BELIEVER! The culture of today is all about getting their brand, their recognition, and their fame. True followers of Christ aren't looking for any of that. Now I'm not saying you're to be a doormat and let others take advantage of you, but you should not be caught up in your way and your rights. Jesus is our example. While He was here on earth He obeyed the Father. He brought no attention to Himself and did not deviate from God's plan. You are saved so you can share your story with others of how God released you from bondage, gave you another chance, and delivered you from eternal separation from God. Everything we have and possess should be put into service for the Lord. As you prayerfully get to know Him and His Will for your life, the Lord will show you how to be a good steward of all you have and bring glory to Him.

6

REMEMBER HIS PROMISES

How many of the following sayings do you know and can complete?

We must not promise what we ought not...

Magnificent promises are always to be...

Don't ever promise more than you can deliver, but always...

Promises are like crying babies in a theater, they should be...

Never make a promise in...

When you promise something...

The promises of yesterday are the...

Never promise more than...

We must not promise what we ought not...

You can't trust a promise someone makes while they're...

So how many did you know? Were you able to guess what came next in each sentence? For those who are curious, I'll have the completed quotes at the end of the chapter. I can honestly say I knew few to none of them. Other than the promises of God, the only promises I'm familiar with are the ones in love songs or poetry. I think if we were to compare notes on jokes about promises, we might do better with what the internet labels famous quotes about promises. One I remember from many years ago is from the animated *Beauty and the Beast* movie where the punished prince is asking what he can do for Belle after her kindness to him. Cogsworth states, "...flowers, chocolates, promises you don't intend to keep." Most of us know promises of that type more than any other.

After doing a simple search in a few Bible commentaries, the consensus was that there are more than eight thousand promises in the Bible with more than seven thousand being specific to people. No matter what the actual number of promises, know when God says something is going to happen, it's going to happen. Period. Since He promised it, He will provide it.

It is very important to note that not all the promises in the Bible are for everyone. This is actually a good thing, so for those of you who like to hoard, this is a helpful thing. Just like we are not given all the spiritual gifts and we aren't to work in every part of the body of Christ at the same time, our desire should be on what He has promised for us specifically. If we were to analyze God's character and how He operates, we'd notice He does things over time, allowing growth and development, so the receiver is ready to receive the promised blessing. As a parent, I always wanted to give my children what they needed when they needed it, not before they were ready. God's promises serve multiple purposes, but for His children, we just need to know He always provides what we need when we need it in just the right amount.

This is difficult to accept sometimes. God is a God of love. God is a God of peace and joy. God is holy and just. He can't lie. He is always faithful and never makes a mistake. Oftentimes we want to superimpose His promises on everything in our lives, forgetting that as a just God, He is going to make sure His will is fulfilled first before He addresses your wish list. Don't set yourself up for defeat and disappointment. He knows how to bless you, He knows with what to bless you, and He knows when to bless you.

So before we get to the good part, let's pause for a moment. There are three enemies when it comes to the promises of God. Satan knows he is lost. His future away from God is sure, so he doesn't care how and when he attacks your mind, your heart, and your spirit. Satan wants you to forget about God's promises to bring you through and bring you out so you'll despair. He wants you to forget about God's promises so you'll try to figure out and fix the issue in your own strength instead of relying on God. The Lord could have just blessed you, just given you an amazing miracle, and Satan would come along in the next moment making you believe you're an orphaned stepchild.

Consider Elijah who had just had one of the greatest victories for God in front of the children of Israel. We can barely start the next chapter, and we see Elijah running, hiding, and wanting to die. I don't want to spoil the story for you, but you have to read 1 Kings chapters 18-19. There was no doubt that God answered in a mighty way. Why in the world did Elijah, a fierce man of God, seem to be running scared for his life? I don't give Elijah a bad time at all. We have all allowed our situation to overwhelm us, forgetting that we have a Father that has everything well in hand. Again, I don't even give the children of Israel a hard time, even though I have a time or two shaken my head or given a side-eye when knowing they had the Lord with them as a cloud by day and a pillar of fire by night, they still couldn't get their act together. Don't think for a minute that it can't happen to you. The devil wants you to walk around defeated and downtrodden. If he succeeds, then you'll take your eyes off Jesus and forget about what God has promised you.

The second enemy of our confidence in God's promises and what we need to guard ourselves regularly against is our flesh, better known as our sinful nature. Our self (flesh) just wants the happy, the pleasure, the quick and easy. Our flesh is only concerned with being satisfied. It is going back to the dust, so the priority of our flesh is only what feels good, even if it's bad for us. It doesn't care how it gets what it wants; it just wants it. If God isn't answering fast enough, our whining and complaining begin. If the answer isn't how or what we desire, we begin to doubt and second-guess the Lord. We even try to help God out by making our own choices, and then we try to have God bless the choices we made. We make promises to the Lord in hopes of getting our way, hoping to bargain our way to what we want.

The third enemy is the world. The world is not our friend. The world would love for us to go away and never talk about our "rules" and our "Jesus." We are to love those in the world and pray for them. We can live in a way to show others a true relationship with Jesus is the only way to God and the only way to have true life. We are all God's creations, but not all of us are God's children. Don't believe me, read about the sheep and goats in Matthew 25:31-46.

I, like most people, didn't understand how promises work and what promises truly are. My first real experience with making a promise was some years earlier. My family had traveled to St. Louis to visit family. The trip was going great, and we all were having a wonderful time. One evening my dad and my uncle Julius took us kids to a baseball game to see the St. Louis Cardinals. We were having a great time, but then my baby sister Renata wandered off and none of us knew where she was. I remember glancing up at the St. Louis Arch and praying one of the sincerest prayers my young heart could make, promising God anything and everything, as long as my little sister was found safe. While my dad and uncle went searching all around the stadium, my other sister DuJuana and I stayed nearby, rechecking the bathroom and concession stands. I kept repeating my prayer over and over again.

My sister and I found her a little later. She was seated with some stadium attendants being spoiled rotten and smiling for all she was worth. Instead of staying with our brother and cousins, she had followed me and my sister when we went to the bathroom without us knowing. After that, we all became more watchful. Even when we returned to California, I continued to be watchful over my siblings, keeping my promise to be more aware of others and what was going on around me.

Even as a child I understood promising something was a big deal. *The Holman Bible Dictionary* defines *promise* this way, "God's announcement of His plan of salvation and blessing to His people, one of the unifying themes integrating the message and the deeds of the Old and New Testaments." Editor Walter C. Kaiser, Jr. continues to explain the word *promise* by discussing the different ways that The Promise is presented first to Abraham and David and then after that, to Jesus with the New Covenant. He ends the section with, "The promise plan of God, then, is indeed His own Word and plan, both in His person and His works, to communicate a blessing to Israel and thereby to bless all the nations of the earth." So God's promises aren't just words to sound pretty or influence us to be good little girls and boys. He is His Promise. Remember God desires a relationship with you. God's promises are not just going to be good possessions to have, but they are going to be Him, the Ultimate Good.

I'm going to talk about seven promises, but realize they are not in any way *the most important* of God's promises. There isn't enough paper and ink to write about all of God's promises. God's promises for provision, His promises for waiting and obeying, and His promises for justice, faith, and protection are just as important. God's promises could be a book all by themselves. I think finding, reading, and studying about God's promises would be a great personal Bible study (hint, hint).

The promises I've selected are going to help us remember the goodness of God. As you spend more time with God He will reveal even more of His promises to you. As I've stated from the beginning, I'm just helping you get started. The Holy Spirit will reveal more and more as you grow in your relationship with the Lord.

The Promise of Salvation

One of the lies the enemy will try to beat you down with is questioning your salvation. *Are you sure you're saved? You've done some bad things. Are you sure you belong to Jesus? You messed up again and you call yourself saved. Are you sure?*

Salvation comes through Jesus Christ. Not your efforts. Not how many times you don't mess up. Not some checklist you keep track of. God knows He is saving imperfect people, which is why He looks at the heart. Even King David knew that "If you seek him, he will be found by you" (1 Chronicles 28:9). The Lord is not trying to play hide-and-seek to keep you away from Him. He wants to save you. He wants to give you the gift of salvation. The Apostle Paul takes us the rest of the way, "If you declare with your mouth, 'Jesus is Lord,' and believe in your heart that God raised him from the dead, you will be saved" (Romans 10:9). Starting your day with time with the Lord where you confess your sins and surrender as you continue to believe in Jesus Christ and what He has done will help in overcoming the lie the enemy wants you to accept. You are His. You will mess up sometimes but don't stay there in the mess. Run to the Lord because only He is the safe place.

The Promise of His Presence

The lies of being alone—you're never going to be supported, or you don't need anyone—have kept many well-meaning Christians weak and anemic. God did not design us to be alone, and He definitely does not want us to do His job. There is a reason that examples of the body are used to describe the church. Hands need legs and feet need eyes. With that said, notice the Lord is always taking care of and providing for the body. He is right there. James 4:8 says, "Come near to God and He will come near to you." He wants us to cry out to Him, especially since He's standing right next to us waiting for us to stop trying to fix the problem and give it to Him. He knows what is happening in the home, church, school, hospital room, courtroom, office, and on the street. Take to heart these words of love from the Lord, "'I will betroth you to me forever; I will betroth you in righteousness and justice, in love and compassion'" (Hosea 2:19). He is not going anywhere, even when we do wrong or choose not to listen to Him, He's still there.

The Promise of Freedom

Discussing freedom can be hard because so many of us are in bondage to things we don't even realize we're in bondage to! When we surrender to the Lord, there is a deliverance that means we are more than conquerors and there are no barriers that can keep up from being all He called us to be.

The Apostle John answers the question of what it means to be set free in Christ in John 8:1-36. The religious leaders are working overtime to try to trap Jesus. People are getting healed and given a chance to have better lives. Religious people are walking around with attitudes and not the nice ones. We can't throw stones at them because we do it too. We're stuck in tradition. We're stuck in culture. We're stuck in trying to make ourselves look better than we truly are. We're stuck trying to please our flesh or seem less abrasive to the world. Sin wants to keep us separated from God and all the blessings He has in store for us. Concerning the promise of freedom, Dr. Charles Stanley answers this way: we are freed from the penalty of sin, released from the power of sin, liberated from the purpose of sin, and unshackled from the personality of sin Jesus promises," 'So if the Son sets you free, you will be free indeed'" (John 8:36). You get to choose God's way. Glory! Glory! Glory!

The Promise of Strength

"I can do all things through Christ, who gives me strength," is not just a placeholder between verses twelve and fourteen when Paul was speaking to the church in Philippi in chapter 4 of Philippians. One of the lies the enemy tells us is we can do it. We're independent. We're strong and capable. We've got this! We trust more in our jobs and bank accounts than we do in regularly practicing relying on the Lord.

Strength is the ability to withstand a great force or pressure. We like to quote, "He won't put more on you than you can bear," when it's someone else going through, but it becomes "woe is me" when we're struggling. Two of my favorite verses are Ephesians 6:13,14, "Therefore put on the full armor of God, so that when the day of evil comes, you may be able to stand your ground, and after you have done everything to stand, Stand firm then..." I actually love that entire book.

Note the Lord didn't lay on Paul's heart for us to build more muscles, eat our vegetables or get the biggest army. He just said to put on the armor and stand. Runners can have heart attacks. Thin people can have horrible diseases. God does not do things the way we think they should go. He wants us to focus completely on Him. Not help Him out. Just stand there because He knows our strength only goes so far and can do only so much. God's strength and power or limitless and never get exhausted. There is no threat of running out when we fully depend on the Lord. Then the enemy wants us to go out on our own. Don't fall for the deception.

Once we stand still and let the Lord fight the battle, the power of the Lord takes over. Power is not strength. We think it is, but, in actuality, power is the source or the supply. God is the source that enables us to overcome and carry out His purposes.

When God used a small boy to save a nation, another small boy to beat a giant, and another small boy's lunch to feed thousands, it wasn't about strength. When God used just a thought or word to heal, restore, or change, it wasn't about strength. Strength gets us part of the way.

When we surrender, fully trust, and obey, things the world defines as weak, the Lord takes those acts of faith and makes us strong by His power. This is why some Christians can endure some of the harshest circumstances. If you didn't know their business, you'd think their lives were sunny and rosy. Look at the first-century Christians. Only God's power could give them the strength to be faithful even at the point of death. He's got that same empowering strength for you, right now. Always available. Always at full capacity. You just need to plug in. Isaiah 40:31 tells us, "But those who hope in the Lord will renew their strength, they will soar on wings like eagles; they will run and not grow weary, they will walk and not be faint."

The Promise of Peace

Notice the Lord didn't promise us a life of no problems, pain, sickness, or heartache. He knew giving us His peace in the midst of the storm would be a blessing. He knew when we chose His peace, we wouldn't be overwhelmed by the trials and tribulations we go through. So many of us have this backward. We somehow read the first part of John 16:33,"'I have told you these things, so that in me you may have peace,'" and miss the rest of the verse, "'In this world you will have trouble. But take heart! I have overcome the world.'"

He speaks to us to prepare us and fill us with His peace. We will have trouble, but then we are to remember that He has overcome the world. We have somehow gotten in our minds that our lives should be peaceful, when in actuality—yes, that word again—we're supposed to be the peace. Our responses and reactions should be so full of God's love that peace can't help but occur.

We are to declare war on Satan and his minions, not on people. People are lost and in bondage. Paul states in Philippians 4:9, "Whatever you have learned or received or heard from me, or seen in me—put it into practice, and the God of peace will be with you." It is not enough just to say the right thing; we have to do the right thing. We don't have to worry. We don't have to doubt. We don't have to have an unsettled heart. The Lord wants us to dwell on His words, "'I will make a covenant of peace with them; it will be an everlasting covenant. I will establish them and increase their numbers, and I will put my sanctuary among them forever'" (Ezekiel 37:26).

The Promise of Joy

Along with the peace comes joy. I don't know about you, but I am so much happier when I've not put more on myself than is necessary. My ministry isn't supposed to look like someone else's ministry. My calling isn't supposed to be exactly like someone else's. That Christian's grass isn't necessarily greener than the grass the Lord has in my yard. The lies of unworthiness or not being good enough are trying to stack up, bombard us, and push us into not believing God and not trusting His process.

Joy allows you to sing with all your heart about the goodness of Jesus even though things don't look good. Joy keeps you praising even though you don't feel like it. When minister Jonathan Evans spoke at his mother's homegoing service in 2020, he demonstrated true joy when he said, "Either she was going to be healed (physically in the body) or she was going to be healed (go home to be with the Lord)." Whew! Sometimes I go to Youtube and pull up his sermonette just to encourage myself!

Have you ever planned a family reunion or a huge function? After all the work you did, didn't you just love it when someone else took the reins the next round, handled everything and all you had to do was show up? Wasn't it just wonderful! God wants to handle everything since He is the only one that can handle everything. We are to trust in the Lord with all our hearts and not lean on our own understanding.

Furthermore, we're to acknowledge the Lord in everything and not depend on our limited understanding. And finally, we're to submit our everything (decision making, agendas, feelings, and emotions) to Him so He can make the path straight, clear, and plain (Proverbs 3:5-7). Hint, hint— read all of Proverbs 3. I'm sure Paul and Silas were putting the proverb into action as they sang and praised God all night in the prison. The joy of the Lord didn't evaporate because of their circumstances. They chose to be bold. If I'm going to suffer then I'm going to suffer for Jesus (Acts 16:16-36).

The Promise of Love

This is a promise the enemy definitely wants us to forget about. God's love is so wonderful, so amazing, so fantastic, the enemy knows that we would indeed be more effective in this dark world if we operated with that truth permeating our entire being. He loves you! There is nothing you can do, even if you reject Him, that would stop Him from loving you. We are the ones that are conditional with our love. I love you if you're doing what we want or are falling in line with our agenda. God doesn't work that way—praise Him for that! Even when eternity starts and those that have chosen to live in eternal darkness, do you realize God still has a love for them? This is why He is always out looking and waiting for any and all to come to him. It was His love that brought Jesus from heaven to earth, to die on the cross and then rise again so we would no longer be separated from God. Romans 5:8 explains, "But God demonstrates his own love for us in this: While we were still sinners, Christ died for us." For God so loved, He said, "Let there be." For God so loved, He said, "Fear not but be strong and courageous." For God so loved, He said, "Follow me." For God so loved, He said, "I am the Alpha and the Omega."

God is not like us; He cannot lie. He wants to give us everything, just like He did with Adam and Eve in the beginning when everything was good. All we need to do is surrender and obey His still small voice that whispers, corrects, and loves.

So daily we have to speak the truth to ourselves and let God's truth get into our spirit. We can put Scripture verses on the mirror, the refrigerator, in our car, in our office desk—everywhere!

Remember:

You are saved

You are never alone, God is *always* with you

You are free!

You will be given strength!

You will have peace

You will have joy

You are loved

Here are the answers to the completed quotes at the beginning of the chapter:

We must not promise what we ought not, lest we be called on to perform what we cannot.

Magnificent promises are always to be suspected.

Don't ever promise more than you can deliver, but always deliver more than you promise.

Promises are like crying babies in a theater; they should be carried out at once.

Never make a promise in haste.

When you promise something, you must fulfill it.

The promises of yesterday are the taxes of today.

Never promise more than you can perform.

We must not promise what we ought not, lest we be called on to perform what we cannot.

You can't trust a promise someone makes while they're drunk, in love, hungry, or running for office.

Let's finish this chapter with a song, an old hymn I remember from my childhood growing up in church.

Standing on the promises of Christ my King,

Through eternal ages let His praises ring,

Glory in the highest, I will shout and sing,

Standing on the promises of God.

Standing, standing,

Standing on the promises of God my Savior;

Standing, standing,

I'm standing on the promises of God.

Standing on the promises that cannot fail,

When the howling storms of doubt and fear assail,

By the living Word of God I shall prevail,

Standing on the promises of God.

Standing on the promises I now can see

Perfect, present cleansing in the blood for me;

Standing in the liberty where Christ makes free,

Standing on the promises of God.

Standing on the promises of Christ the Lord,

Bound to Him eternally by love's strong cord,

Overcoming daily with the Spirit's sword,

Standing on the promises of God.

Standing on the promises I shall not fall,

List'ning every moment to the Spirit's call.

Resting in my Savior as my All in all,

Standing on the promises of God.

Russell Kelso Carter, Standing on the Promises, 1886

HEY NEW BELIEVER! This is one chapter the devil does not want you to take to heart. You may have made promises to the Lord when you gave your life to Him. Some of those promises you may have kept and others might be a struggle. The enemy wants to remind you that you have failed and messed up again. The enemy wants you to think about God in the way that you would think about yourself. Listen up beloved, the Lord never goes back on His Word. Never! He loves you! He has forgiven you and He'll forgive you again. He will not withdraw His love. He patiently waits for you to bring all the broken pieces of your life so He has put you back together. You are free, you are no longer bound. You are not alone, the Lord will always be with you! You will have peace as He strengthens you. You will be surrounded by His love and peace as He brings all He promised to pass.

7

REMEMBER IT'S ALREADY DONE

Do you like knowing how something is going to end? Or do you like surprises or being surprised? Or maybe you're the third category that likes controlled surprises? In the late 1970s and early 1980s *Choose Your Own Adventure Books* were very popular. I remember reading a few in elementary school. Some books had as many as thirty-eight options before getting to the end. I never found that particular book. I always seemed to choose the short version and my story ended quickly.

After a few times of not getting some of the endings my classmates got, I stopped reading those types of books altogether. Unfortunately, this also caused me to sometimes look at the last chapter of books. I like happy endings or at least a story where the bad guy gets punished. I didn't always turn to the end of the book, but I avoided these books when I went to the library. By the time I went to high school, I learned to just take books chapter by chapter and enjoy or sometimes endure the story.

Have you ever skipped to the end of a book or movie to see how it ended? How about have you ever rewatched or reread something that you considered a favorite because you already knew how it was going to end? I rarely skipped ahead on something I enjoyed. I wanted to enjoy every moment. Now something that was a bit boring or was taking too long to get to the point? I might skip a few pages, or in the good ole days, I would push the fast-forward button on the VCR to get to the good part or the end. With streaming services, blue ray, and DVDs, skipping ahead takes on a whole different meaning. I've heard people wish they could fast-forward through times in their lives, skipping past what they didn't like and only stopping at the good parts.

OH LORD I FORGOT AGAIN!

When I was fifteen years old, I got chicken pox. It was dreadful. I was sicker than my siblings, once they got it, except for my baby sister who got really ill too. But it was awful. It wasn't just the itching and discomfort, but the fact that all of my skin was covered.

After two weeks my suffering wasn't done. My skin became even more sensitive and I had hives for another two weeks. I was in driver's training class, and you were only allowed ten absences or you would have to repeat the entire class. Thankfully it was my first-period class, so I would go to that class and then go home. The hives were so bad it looked like someone was beating me. This would be the beginning of my strawberry and avocado allergies. During this time I was imagining and dreaming about this all being over. It took time, but the chicken pox and hives were gone. Eventually, my skin was back to normal, and I didn't have any more issues, but it took time. No amount of wishing it was all over made the healing process go any faster.

We do this spiritually sometimes as we try to rush the Lord. We are so quick to get to the blessing, not realizing we need to be learning during the process to get to the blessing. Unlike the books where we can pick which page to turn to, we must let the Lord write the chapters of our lives. He has already done everything that needs to be done. We are the ones that are catching up.

As we wrap up our time together I pray you are encouraged to remember He has saved you, always has strength for you, and continually gives you His power to have peace, joy, and love so you can experience true freedom in Christ.

One of the best ways to end is with the beginning. Let's look at some key verses in Genesis:

Genesis 1:1, "In the beginning God created the heavens and the earth."

Genesis 1:31a, "God saw all that He had made, and it was very good."

Genesis 2:2-3, "By the seventh day God had finished the work he had been doing; so on the seventh day he rested from all his work. Then God blessed the seventh day and made it holy because on it he rested from all the work of creating that he had done."

God knew exactly what He was doing when He started creating and designing the world and the universe. Nothing that has happened or will happen has caught Him off guard. I can't imagine the sadness the Lord's heart must have when looking at the state of our world. But even in that He has already worked everything out and prepped it to turn around to give Him glory. This isn't an easy fact for even seasoned Christians to accept. We want the Garden of Eden now. Sorry, that's not one of the promises. Plus, if He gave us all that He did at the beginning when everything was good, what would He have for us once we get to heaven? 1 Corinthians 2:9 tells us, "However, as it is written: What no eye has seen, what no ear has heard, and what no human mind has conceived, the things God has prepared for those who love him."

I take great comfort in knowing that God has a prepared place for me and you. He isn't getting it ready or just drawing up the plans. It is done. When Jesus said it was finished, God had already organized where we would spend eternity with Him. This is another reason why none of us should shy away from the Book of Revelation. The Apostle John obediently reminds us in Revelation 1:3, "Blessed is the one who reads aloud the words of this prophecy, and blessed are those who hear it and take to heart what is written in it, because the time is near."

Everything is unfolding as it is supposed to. I know this is another hard-to-swallow fact. "I am the Alpha and the Omega, says the Lord God, who is, and who was, and who is to come, the Almighty," (Revelation 1:8). God covered all bases, past, present, and future. This means you can trust Him to heal you of your past, carry you in your present, and preserve you in your future.

Let's look at some ways we can remember that the Lord has already done all that needs to be done.

Live by Faith

Let's start with one of the key verses about faith: Hebrews 11:1, "Now faith is confidence in what we hope for and assurance about what we do not see." Faith is one of the first actions we do when we first accept Jesus Christ. By faith, we believe He came to earth via virgin birth, lived a sinless life, went to the cross, died, and then rose three days later. By faith, we know the Lord will come through even though we cannot see it. By faith, we know the Lord will make a way even though it's dark, obscure, and seemingly impossible. By faith, we don't rely on our feelings, emotions, and so-called knowledge. By faith, we take God's Word as inspired Scripture and accept that God does not change. By faith, we know we please God when we live by faith and not by sight (2 Corinthians 5:7). By faith, we are crucified with Christ and now have a new life we live by faith in the Son of God who loves us and gave Himself for us (Galatians 2:20). We can be encouraged, "For in the gospel the righteousness of God is revealed—a righteousness that is by faith from first to last, just as it is written: 'The righteous will live by faith'" (Romans 1:17).

Continue to Grow Spiritually

1 Corinthians 13:11, "When I was a child, I talked like a child, I thought like a child, I reasoned like a child. When I became a man, I put the ways of childhood behind me." The Apostle Paul tells us that we should not look the same spiritually year after year after year. Growth means we get a little closer to the Lord in some way. We are relying more on the Lord. In the area we are struggling with, we turn to God first rather than the fifth time around. We yearn to spend more time with Him than with anyone else or doing anything else. We search out more ways to please Him and let our lives be a praise to Him.

Colossians 1:10 reflects this idea, "So that you may live a life worthy of the Lord and please Him in every way; bearing fruit in every good work, growing in the knowledge of God."

It's not about the works but about our love and gratefulness for Jesus' sacrifice that motivates us to grow to look more like Him and less like ourselves. As we walk by faith, we'll grow more and more. Just as we have a birthday each year, we should have a spiritual birthday each year as well. The same things that made us angry last year should not make us mad this year or at least not as angry. Our buttons are not pushed as readily.

Our agenda or the selfish way we want things to be done do not take center stage. Here's a cautionary verse: "He cuts off every branch in me that bears no fruit, while every branch that does bear fruit He prunes so that it will be even more fruitful" (John 15:2),

Be Filled with the Spirit

Acts 2:4, "All of them were filled with the Holy Spirit and began to speak in other tongues as the Spirit enabled them." Notice anywhere in Scripture, Old Testament or New Testament, the Lord always filled whomever He was using with His Spirit. Being filled with the Spirit is what you want before anything you do, anywhere you go, anything you might say. Before a decision has to be made. Before a change has to happen. When the Spirit fills the place and the people, the impossible becomes possible. The improbable becomes probable. The ordinary becomes extraordinary. This is why Paul and Silas could praise God while in prison. This is why the prophet Nathan could stand before King David and expose his sin. This is why Joshua was able to lead the Israelites into the Promised Land. Remember it's not about you but about the Lord working in and through you, as we're reminded in this verse: "Since we live by the Spirit, let us keep in step with the Spirit" (Galatians 3:25).

Put All Your Trust in the Lord

Psalm 56:11, "In God I trust and am not afraid. What can man do to me?" Trust is a tough one, especially since we rely on our human experiences with each other to decide just how much or how little we trust God. Trust is that opportunity to put your faith, growth, and filling of the Spirit to work. When we trust, we pray, *Lord, I don't know how You are going to do it, but I know that You will bring me out and through this situation. I will have joy and peace as I demonstrate love and patience with those who would seek to destroy me.*

Trust is saying, *Even if You do not heal me, You will be with me.* Trust is, *Even if I don't get the job, You will meet all my needs according to Your riches in glory.* Trust is staying in that job you'd like to leave because He's not done with you being His ambassador there. Trust is leaving that job even when one may not be on the horizon because God is allowing you to rest before He puts you in the next strategic place He wants to use you. Trust is a process, but like anything you have to actively participate. Here's a promise about trust: "May the God of hope fill you with all joy and peace as you trust in Him, so that you may overflow with hope by the power of the Holy Spirit" (Romans 15:13).

Surrender to the Lord Daily

Romans 12:1, "Therefore, I urge you, brothers and sisters, in view of God's mercy, to offer your bodies as a living sacrifice, holy and pleasing to God—this is your true and proper worship." I love how the King James Version says, "...present your bodies a living sacrifice, holy acceptable unto God, which is your reasonable service." Reasonable! God's perspective on surrender is not the same as how the world tries to portray it as if you're a loser or invaluable. Like trust, we often have a hard time surrendering. In actuality, when you surrender, the pressure is off you. You have handed over the keys to the car, and you have gotten in the backseat, put your seatbelt on, and kept your mouth shut on how to drive the car. It is you recognizing God is in control, and your attempt to be in control has come to an end. Proverbs 3:6 states, "Trust in the Lord with all your heart and lean not on your own understanding; in all your ways submit to him, and he will make your paths straight." We can quote Proverbs 3:5-6, but to truly trust in the Lord, we have to surrender. To truly not lean on our own understanding, we have to surrender. To acknowledge Him in everything, we have to surrender. The more you surrender to the filling of the Holy Spirit, the more you grow, the more you will trust, and the more stepping out in faith you will do. Surrender means you pray Psalm 51, the Scripture of forgiveness and restoration, over yourself. Surrender means you declare all of Romans chapter 8, the Apostle Paul's encouraging words and admonitions about life through the Spirit, over your life. Surrender means you believe this verse: "We are hard pressed on every side, but not crushed; perplexed, but not in despair; persecuted, but not abandoned; struck down, but not destroyed" (2 Corinthians 4:8-9).

Your Purpose Is Clear

2 Timothy 2:21," Those who cleanse themselves from the latter will be instruments for special purposes, made holy, useful to the Master and prepared to do any good work." As you pray without ceasing and seek the kingdom of God, your purpose becomes clearer. Just like Abram left all he knew and got a new name and a new location, you'll say, *Lord, I'll be like Abram and do what You want.* I'll serve Him here or there. I will serve Him everywhere. I am saved to serve. *Lord send me, I'll go.* As you keep surrendering your wants, desires, dreams, and life pursuits, you grow to see things as God sees things. You let the Holy Spirit fill you as you trust Him to send you where He needs you to be, walking by faith and trusting Him to make the increase as you plant the seeds

of righteousness. Remember your calling. Put on the armor of God and stand. Remember to follow the instructions. You'll walk in the light of this verse: "'But I have raised you up for this very purpose, that I might show you my power and that my name might be proclaimed in all the earth'" (Exodus 9:16).

The Victory Is Sure

1 Corinthians 15:57, "But thanks be to God! He gives us the victory through our Lord Jesus Christ." The Lord has given you the victory. Say that out loud—the Lord has given you the victory. Despite what your current situation might be, the Lord has already provided the victory.

Want to know why the world gives Christians such a hard time? In our effort to fit in, be nonabrasive, and get along, we walk around defeated and discouraged more than the world. We are subdued and disheartened as if Jesus is still in the grave. We serve a risen Savior! He defeated death! He conquered sin! We can proclaim, *Victory shall be mine if I hold my peace and let the Lord fight my battle.* If you never get your prayers answered the way you want them to be answered, you still have the victory. Your victory in Jesus is a sure thing! Whatever you think the highest honor is —Nobel prize, Oscar, Grammy, Tony, Olympic Gold medal, World record breaker, Stanley Cup, World Series, Superbowl, Championship, or Hall of Fame induction— these pale in comparison to the victory we have in Jesus.

As we continue to step out in faith, grow in Christ, and are filled with the Holy Spirit, continually trusting and surrendering to the Lord's purpose for our life, we stand with our heads held high even when our hearts are heavy. We walk around victorious, not putting on a show for the world, but walking in confidence because of who God is. We're saying, *It might look like we're losing, but God's got the victory and I will share in it.* We'll be able to state, *Things aren't perfect because the Lord said in this world we will have trouble. But I don't have to be worried, scared, or depressed because I am in the safest place. The King of Kings and Lord of Lords is handling my well-being and all my needs.* God promises us, "'To the one who is victorious, I will give the right to sit with me on my throne, just as I was victorious and sat down with my Father on his throne'" (Revelation 3:21).

If you want to be good at something or successful in a task, you have to repeat the actions needed more than once. Words such as *without ceasing*, *daily*, and *continually* are there as markers for us to focus on Jesus and His perfect will for our lives. You don't have to know how it is going to end specifically. You can still know that God is only going to give you what is good and perfect. The Lord has given the ending to you already. He wins, so we win! We don't have to be in a hurry, unless it's to share the Good News with everyone, everywhere, every chance we get.

Here's our list to help us remember that the Lord has already accomplished everything and we can thrive victoriously:

Live by faith

Grow spiritually

Be filled with the Spirit

Put your trust in the Lord

Surrender to the Lord

Your purpose is clear

Your victory is sure

Before I pray I have one more **Hey New Believer!** Remembering that God has already done everything He wants to do is a life-long process. We are on a step-by-step journey and are moving toward what God has already made perfect. This is not a make-a-wish and wait-for-it-to-happen type of situation. The Lord wants us to walk by faith and live with joyous expectation each day He gives us. This is not easy, even for the seasoned believer. The Lord is not looking for you to be perfect. He doesn't need a performance from you. He just wants you to surrender to Him. He just wants you to trust Him and obey His Words. Everything will fall into place and be worth the sacrifice. Don't give up. Don't let go of the Lord's hand.

Thank you for joining me in this journey of remembering. I hope these words will continue to be an encouragement to you. Join me in praying:

Lord,

I just praise You for being God. I thank you for not making a mistake and never breaking a promise to any of us. Thank you, Lord, for being an omnipotent, omniscient, and omnipresent God that cares about little ole me. I am humble each day knowing You desire a relationship with me. Help me to remember that I belong to You and only You. No one can take me from Your hands. Help me to remember that You brought me out and will bring me through and out of every trouble and situation that I will experience. I am more than a conqueror through You.

Lord, I thank You for Your Word and how it speaks to me every day. Help me to remember to seek out Your work and instructions daily in every area of my life. Again, Lord, I am humbled that You don't need me but chose to use me and have called and anointed me to be Your servant. Help me to remember my calling and treat Your precious gift to me with reverence and devotion. Lord, thank you for Your mercy, grace, and forgiveness. I have been selfish and unkind, but You have continued to bless and keep me. You corrected and guided me in the way You wanted me to go. Help me to remember that it is not about me but all about You. Thank you, Lord, for Your promises which demonstrate the amazing depths of Your love.

May I spend less time being forgetful of Your goodness and more mindful that You've got me securely in Your hands and that You have already done it all! It is handled. It is complete. May my life be a sweet fragrance of worship and praise as I obey You and leave the consequences up to You.

In Jesus' Mighty Name,

Amen and Amen.

WORKS CITED

Butler, T. C., PH.D. *Holman Bible Dictionary*. Holman Bible Publishers, 1991.

Dahl, Roald. Charlie and the Chocolate Factory. Puffin Books, 1964.

Stanley, C. F. *The Charles F. Stanley Life Principles Bible* (2nd ed.). Thomas Nelson, 2009.

Warren, Rick. *God's Power to Change Your Life*. Zondervan, 2014.

"What does it mean to walk by faith? Got Questions Ministries, accessed October 1, 2019, from https://www.gotquestions.org/walk-by-faith-not-by-sight.html

ARE YOU A NEW BELIEVER?

Did you accept the Lord as your personal Lord and Savior? We'd love to hear about it! You can drop us a message at www.klensor.com[1]. We encourage you to tell someone and join your local Bible-believing and teaching church. Below are resources from Bible ministers and teachers that seek to proclaim Jesus Christ and reach out to others:

In Touch Ministries

www.intouch.org/topics/new-believers[2]

The Urban Alternative Ministries

tonyevans.org/jesus

Daily Hope Ministries

pastorrick.com/know-god

Harvest Ministries

harvest.org/request-material

---

1. http://www.klensor.com
2. http://www.intouch.org/topics/new-believers

ACKNOWLEDGEMENTS

Huge thank you to all my prayer partners and my family for all their support. Special thanks to my Power Team: Beverly Dennis, Samuel Dennis, Kathy Logue, Mary Logue, Denise Nelson, Julie Sweeney, DuJuana Ware, and Retta Ware; your input and feedback have been invaluable. Thank you to Valerie J. Lewis easy to follow mentoring and my Pen of the Writer cohorts for being there and your encouragement. Thank you to Flourish Writers for the inspiration to turn this work into a Bible study. And last but definitely not least I thank Almighty God for leading and guiding me through this entire journey.

ABOUT THE AUTHOR

KL Ensor is a writer, speaker, and author that loves sharing God's Word. She connects with readers by sharing life lessons and adventures from her personal walk with the Lord, illustrating the goodness, faithfulness, and unfailing love of God when we give our lives over to Him completely. Drawing on experiences as a wife, mom, teacher, and nurse, she offers encouragement and support to reinforce the fact that God loves you, He desires you to trust Him and follow His plan for your life no matter what. KL Ensor and her husband have been married since 1994 and have two children. She is currently attending Bible College working toward ordination.

KL Ensor

8898 Navajo Road #C314

San Diego, CA 92119

619-461-2169

www.klensor.com[1]

---

1. http://www.klensor.com